Once A
Warrior

Hawai'i Football, On the Field and Off the Record

Once A Warrior

Hawai'i Football, On the Field and Off the Record

BY J. IAN SAMPLE

WATERMARK
PUBLISHING

ISBN 978-0-9790647-9-1

Library of Congress Control Number: 2007934966

Design
Leo Gonzalez

Production
Herlinda Lopez

Watermark Publishing
1088 Bishop Street, Suite 310
Honolulu, HI 96813
Telephone: Toll-free 1-866-900-BOOK
Web site: www.bookshawaii.net
email: sales@bookshawaii.net

Printed in the United States

CONTENTS

ACKNOWLEDGMENTS

Thanks must go out...

To my teammates and especially to my receivers. I have to watch the games over again to really remember what it was like—the cheers, the screams, the fanfare. Those parts were good but they were only the milieu. You few guys made this football thing worthwhile. At clubs I'd wait for a fight to break out so I'd have a chance to show my dedication, my loyalty to you guys. In the game I'd pray that I'd have the opportunity to throw a big block, especially against a lineman or linebacker so you'd see what I'd put on the line for one of you. But that chance never came and already a new season has begun. I've missed my opportunity and with the inevitability of time some of us will grow apart and fade away— I guess that's only natural. But whatever you're doing come five, 10 years from now, know that you had a teammate—you have a friend—who's loyalty will remain as timeless as these words. Thank you.

To Brian Wong, Eric Okasaki, Jay-Goo, Renae, Nikki, Karen, Vanessa and the rest of the Makai training staff who tried so hard to keep this body of mine healthy. But more than that, thanks for making the training room my home away from home—my sanity was saved within your walls.

To Al, Sudsy, Atsu and Uncle Mike, for bringing a much-needed laugh after a shitty practice.

To my Virgils of the book world—Stephanie Miller, Sarah Nunes-Atabaki, Susan Schultz, Lance Tominaga, Chari Cortez, George Engebretson, Aimee Harris and Elinor Nauen. To Steven Colbert and his Report—your Tivo'd shows keep me awake while I attempt to make history.

To Michelle and Charlie who had to endure the late-night pounding on the keyboard.

To my landlords who double as my great friends—Kat, Shaundra, Regan and Emilee, thank you so much for the roof over my head but, more important, for your companionship.

To Dutch, C-dawg, Apryle, Ike, Cake, Ernest, Flower, Em Rose, Nolan, Zach and hundreds of others who have moved me in Hawai'i.

To the Dove Family for being real family.

To GG, GJ, Grandma Parker, Grandma Nora, Aunt B, Aunt Wincey, Uncle Tommy, Tony, Uncle Daryl, Princess, Ryan, Stefon, Uncle Tommy and Aunt Pat for the years of undying love. I soak it up and although I'm bad at expressing it, it fuels me way more than I've let on. Thank you.

To Marc, Matt, Corey Andrew and Chris, who will forever serve as my foundation back in the 201.

To Cassiel and Uncle Steve for their help in opening my eyes and heart to the "impossible"— I will continue my journey.

To Mom, Dad, Travis, Nikki and Ryan for the absolute essentials—love, affection, faith and cheers.

To the one who has done all the above—Koren Takeyama. Kor, without you I'd be living on the streets, with but a penny in my pocket and no affection in my heart. Thank you so very much, my heffer; this book is yours as much as mine.

I shiver in my dreams and wake to grab a shooting star.
Then make a wish to dream again
—Alas, my dreams not far.

Thanks, Dad, for allowing me to dream.

INTRODUCTION

TO BE A WARRIOR

Behind the smoke and mirrors there lies an ancient game far more complex than what is seen on TV. Once you dissolve all the illusions and facades, you begin to see a change: What was once a brutish game of kill-or-be-killed is now an intricate lifestyle, serving as a perfect microcosm for life itself.

That's how I answered a friend who asked me why I was writing a book about football. If you can wade through the gaudy rhetoric, you'll find one reason why I think football is important. But that's only part of the story.

So why am I writing a book about football? More than a few people have asked me that. I mean, it's not like I live and breathe the sport. When I'm not at practice or on the field on game day, I don't even think much about it. Whenever I can, I enjoy escaping from the world of whistles, first downs and penalties. Never in my constant inner monologue do I call myself, "Ian the football player." More often, I'm "Ian the aspiring scholar" or, when I'm feeling really ambitious, "Ian the budding philanthropist."

I always thought that a "real" football player was a guy who couldn't live without the sport. You know the type—always watching *Sports Center* when he isn't working out or actually playing, the guy with his team's colors plastered all over the house. In college he's the player who has no answer to the question, "What are you going to do with your life if football doesn't work out?" But the more I think about it, the more I realize that I am indeed a "real" player. I've been playing the game since the second grade and all the while, football has woven itself into the very fabric of who I am.

From the very first time I pulled on a helmet and called myself a Falcon, I was a football player. For those four great high school years as a Cardinal, when I helped my team win a state championship and was named New Jersey's first-team all-state defensive back, I was a football player. And even for the one semester I spent as a Fightin' Blue Hen for the University of Delaware, I was a football player.

But not until I stepped on the field as a University of Hawai'i Warrior did I realize that football is far more than a game—it is life. It isn't life in the sense that there is nothing else out there, but rather because it is a constant journey. And like life itself, it is unfair, forever changing and often out of your control.

That's a lesson I started learning as soon as I graduated from high school in 2001 and signed a letter of intent to play for Delaware on a full-ride football scholarship. I redshirted in my freshman year; that is, I practiced but didn't play in any games to save a year of eligibility. But after football season, I dropped out of school and returned home to Jersey to help a family member in need. I spent more than a year at home, taking night classes at community college and working part-time at a local grocery store. So here I was, the one-time all-state football star and senior class president, back home without a single claim to fame— besides the fact that I could bag groceries so that your eggs wouldn't crack, even at the bottom of the sack. I felt like my life had taken a 180, and I wasn't quite sure where I was headed. But for the first time in my life I practiced a valuable skill. It wasn't catching, running or even lifting; it was patience. I tried to make the best of my situation—for example, it gave me the time to watch my 13-year-old brother grow.

Then, after more than a year, things began looking up. My high-light tapes had come to the attention of Rich Miano, the walk-on coach at the University of Hawai'i, a program gaining national attention for its pass-intensive, run-and-shoot offense under Coach June Jones. With Coach Miano's help, I officially became a Warrior in the fall of 2003 and made the 5,000-mile move from Jersey to Honolulu. I was able to practice that season but, due to National Collegiate Athletic Association (NCAA) transfer rules, I wasn't allowed to participate in any games. My first year was a humbling experience—as a one-time all-state scholarship player who now had to work his way up from the very bottom. However, by the 2004 season, my junior year, I was getting into the rotation at wide receiver, and by the fifth game I was switching in and out with the starter. But in that game, as I was finally getting the experience I needed, I dove for a ball in the back of the end zone and suddenly found myself sidelined for the rest of the season with a broken collarbone. Once again, I was playing the waiting game.

Another spring and summer passed and I was already a fifth-year senior with just one final season to play. I had been able to work my way up from lowly walk-on to full scholarship starter. Surrounding me were a new but very skilled group of receivers, and leading the way was a young and talented quarterback by the name of Colt Brennan. Yet no sooner had the season started than the unfairness of football jumped up and grabbed me by the knee. I suffered yet another season-ending injury—this time a tear in a ligament at the back of my knee.

I had spent five hard years dedicating myself to college football and had played in only seven games. I had prepared, trained and waited, and all I had to show for it was seven semi-productive days in autumn. Lucky for me, football is governed by certain rules that in extreme circumstances can offer a second chance—or in my case, a sixth chance. Because my injuries had taken me away from the game for so long, I was able to appeal to the NCAA for one more year of playing eligibility. After much deliberation, I was granted a sixth year. That year was the 2006 UH Warrior football season, a magical, record-breaking season of lopsided scores, fan frenzy and a national Top 25 ranking.

But I still haven't answered the question: Why write a book? It's partly because the story of that watershed season—and especially the story behind the season—is worth telling. It's partly because the opinions of my fellow Warriors—opinions seldom aired in a public forum—deserve to be read. In these pages, you'll read about Game Day—14 of them, actually—with special emphasis on the receiver corps, central figures in the Warrior's pass-happy offense. But you'll also find anecdotes here about Warrior life off the field—on the sidelines, in the locker room, on the road, in the clubs.

For my teammates and me, this is our way of sharing just what it means to be a Warrior. It isn't something that ends when the clock runs out on the final game of your senior season. The fact is: once a Warrior, always a Warrior.

And if these stories or opinions offend anyone—fan or foe—well, that's the risk I take. It's something any writer faces. As Salman Rushdie put it, "What is freedom of expression? Without the freedom to offend, it ceases to exist."

Enjoy.

PROLOGUE

BEGINNING AT THE END

Christmas Eve, 2006. The Sheraton Hawaiʻi Bowl. For us seniors, it was our final game—the last time we'd walk through the tunnel wearing our Warrior fatigues. This game meant everything to us. It wasn't because of our opponent, Arizona State, as we'd seen far worthier teams. It meant everything because this game was the culmination of an epic season—a season headlined by record-breaking moments and immaculate plays. For those who knew Warrior Football, they also knew that the words "team," "Hawaiʻi" and "Warrior" were far more than just ink on a page. Those words, roughly translated, meant "family."

With thousands of fans and friends watching, we wanted to leave everything on the field. We hoped to play until the final seconds ticked away and the whistle blew, ending the game and our illustrious season. But for me, the storybook ending would have to come at some other time, in some other form. Instead of a final whistle bringing my collegiate career to a close, it ended at halftime with a single word, "No." Let me take you back to the first quarter so you can follow me through the series of events leading up to that career-ending word.

My first reception came after I ran a quick screen. I didn't get very far and the ball was stripped away. I didn't remember falling down, but I do remember feeling a shooting pain in my foot. Someone must have stepped on it. I thought I'd run it off. But the more I ran the more it hurt. At each play I released off the line slower and slower. I couldn't even get past the corner without wincing in pain. But my pride had the best of me. This was my very last game. I needed to stay in.

With the first quarter over, we were already down 3-0. Our defense was holding strong, but on countless occasions, our offense failed to reach the end zone. With the start of the second quarter we needed new life, and on this one particular drive we were determined to finally put up some points. We were already deep in Sun Devil territory and looking to score. I ran a short pattern across the middle. Colt Brennan, our quarterback, was scrambling so I cut back out to the sideline to mirror his direction. The moment I cut I heard a pop in my foot. It took me a second, but I pushed through the pain and continued with my pattern. The ball was in the air and I knew I was wide open with nothing but end zone behind me. I saw the ball coming and I dropped it! I'd dropped balls in my career before. Some were hard to catch, others I dropped because of nerves, but most of them because I was thinking of my next move. But never in my life had I dropped a ball with no explanation. Even now I'd like to blame my foot or find some other excuse for why I dropped what would have been my final collegiate touchdown. But I can't find one. My eyes were on it, and I saw everything around me. Wide receiver Davone Bess was right ahead of me, and I knew my cornerback had overplayed his pursuit to the right. When the ball slipped through my hands I turned to see the unguarded path to the end zone. I dropped my head down in dismay. I quickly tried to forget about it. I told myself to one-snap and clear it. As I jogged back to the huddle I felt a sharp pain coming from my foot. I was lucky because the pain overshadowed my disappointment and disbelief.

I went in at halftime and the doctors took an X-ray of my foot. No broken bones. The docs asked if I could run on it, I told them no. It looked as if I was out for the game. I quickly asked if they could shoot it up. Numb it. I so desperately needed a chance at redemption. The docs agreed and soon after they administered the shot I got back on the field and jogged around. The shot alleviated enough of the pain. I could play. Besides, I had already suffered a slipped disc, broken bones, torn ligaments and countless muscle tears. There was no way a sprained foot was going to keep me out.

I jogged up to head coach June Jones and asked if I could go back in. He didn't look at me; he just said, "No." No? I thought to myself. Because I dropped the ball? Other receivers have dropped far more important balls than that. Did he think I couldn't get the job done? Had he not counted on me on crucial third and fourth downs time and time again? Had he lost confidence in my ability? Have I not shown enough will and heart this past season to keep me in? I was irate! If someone had asked me that very instant what I thought of Coach Jones, I would have tossed out every four-letter word in the book! I sat on the bench and took a deep, long breath. I knew there was nothing I could do.

I was oblivious to the rest of the game. It went on without me, just as I knew it would. I don't remember Jason Rivers' touchdowns or Nate

Ilaoa's great runs. I can't recall Davone's two personal fouls leading to his ejection. As the game, with all of its cheers and boos, danced in the back of my mind, I thought about how I got to playing football. Within a matter of minutes, as I sat there trying to repress my anger, I recapped an entire season. I thought about all the practices and game highlights, and everything else that happened on and off the gridiron. I thought about how the touchdowns and tackles highlighted on K5's newscasts and in the newspapers are only a small part of the game. To its players, football is more about what happens off the field and off the record. The truth of the game lies in the locker room and behind other closed doors, where coaches can't curb our thoughts and the media can't twist our words. That is truly when football, to us players, is life.

As the clock wound down, I thought back to how my season had started. It was early August, and the same man who'd just ended my college career came into the film room and said, "Ian, we just heard ... you're cleared to play."

CHAPTER 1

SUMMER CAMP

The Dreaded 220s

I waited for what felt like years to find out if I was cleared to play. I was appealing to the National College Athletic Association (NCAA) for a sixth year of eligibility. Our starting running back, Nate Ilaoa, and safety Leonard Peters joined me in making sixth-year appeals to the NCAA. However, it was August 4th and summer camp had begun already. I couldn't do anything but show up. Real practice hadn't started yet so I wasn't missing anything important—just orientation programs and playbook learning. It wasn't until the day before the 220 test when Coach Jones entered the film room and asked, "Is Ian here?"

I was sitting with the rest of the receivers and replied, "Right here, Coach."

"Ian, we just heard …you're cleared to play," he said.

I said thanks, and just turned around and smiled. I had waited for nearly a year for those words. I was now part of the team, officially. Davone made some comment like, "Wipe the shit-eating grin off your face." I just laughed. I couldn't stop smiling. But I'd have an entire season to celebrate this great news. Now it was time to really start focusing on football. And what a great time to get cleared, the day before our 220 test. Shit!

There is nothing fun about running, unless you enjoy the gut-wrenching feeling of last night's plate lunch slowly rising up in your throat and the loss of sensation in your lower extremities. The chief motivating factors behind running are: a) beating other people, b) knowing you are getting faster and c) participating in what can be the most competitive event between football players—running. Keep in mind, of course, that I am coming from a receiver's perspective, so running holds more weight, if not all the weight, for my position.

Mention 220s around any of the bigger guys, especially the line-

men, and you will see the fear in their eyes! This is our real test at summer camp. We have to run 110 yards, touch a line and then go back 110
yards. Hence, the 220 test. We have to perform 10 220s within a set time.
The linemen are given the most time, followed by the linebackers. Then
the skill positions run with the least amount of time. Needless to say, no
matter what the group or time, the test is no walk in the park. The 220s
reveal who's in shape to the coaches and also answers by default the
question, "Who's serious about football this season?"

Running or doing anything physical to the point of exhaustion is a
great way to divide the team. And I mean this in a good way because it
quickly shows where lie the proverbial mice and men. The mice squeak,
"We'll never have to run 200 yards in a game! Why are we doing this?"
"This is so stupid," "Man, I'm just going to jog this one." Meanwhile, the
men have a different attitude toward things: "Come on, push it, keep
it going," "Three more to go, stand tall, we can do this." The men are
encouraging, they know what they have to do and just do it. It's during
the running that a player's fortitude is weighed. The 220s also show the
coaches how deep we can dig.

I do believe that some of the mice are justified in their complaints,
especially when they say that a specific run or workout has no real foot-
ball-related benefits. However, as members of a team, they must realize
they are going to have to do things they don't want to. They also have to
realize that negativity is like cancer—it's quick to spread.

Workouts differ from school to school, team to team and athlete
to athlete. With that said, the goal of any program is to make sure its
athletes are getting stronger, faster and better. But ultimately, the ambi-
tion to become great depends solely upon the athlete. Since each person
is built differently and has different weaknesses and strengths, it's up
to the individual to supplement his assigned workouts. As players on a
team, we first must do what is required by our coaches and then add on
whatever else is necessary to excel.

The biggest element missing from the Warrior workout was posi-
tion-specific training. Different positions call for a range of skills and
muscle performance. Although, the proper adjustments should have
been made to our lifting program, they were not. This is when an ambitious player would pull aside a strength coach, such as Tommy Heffernan
or DeJuan Hathaway, and ask them, "Hey, what can I do to increase my

vertical?" or "What will it take to shave seconds off my 40?" With this type of drive, the last separation from within a team is made—from mice and men, leaders are found.

The Quest to be #1

Tensions flare when summer camp comes around. Energy runs high and so does competitiveness. While time-proven players such as Leonard Peters or our big center, Samson Satele, already know they have nothing to lose at camp, others still need to prove their worth to their coaches and peers. As football players we have to set up goals for ourselves. From the second we walk onto the practice field, there are others who will try to hold us back from attaining these goals. Yet we all hope that through hard work and dedication, we'll all become prized starting players.

Typically there are four different kinds of players who aim at becoming a starter. Each one differs, from voracity to experience, but until summer camp has ended any one of them could get the job. It's not where you line up," Coach Jeff Reinebold liked to say, "it's where you wind up."

The first group are the freshman and transfers. These wide-eyed individuals are usually the most outspoken. They come in two waves; the junior college kids stroll in sometime in January for the spring semester, while almost all the freshman come in for August's fall camp. No matter when they arrive, their debut is accented by arrogance and cockiness. "I ran the 40-yard dash in 4.35 seconds." "My vertical is 42 inches." "I had one game where I juked out five players and ran in for my fifth touchdown of the game." So much talk! They will brag about everything and claim that they were 'the man' in high school. The way they talk about themselves, it seems that every one of them should've gone to a football powerhouse like Florida or Ohio State. Often, these players have the most ability but are the least prepared for the responsibility. It would be like throwing a sign-language expert into a traffic cop's job. With his fast and effective hands, he'd be an exceptional candidate for the job, but he doesn't understand the flow of traffic. He isn't sure where to stand or even which way the traffic should be moving. Likewise, the freshmen and transfers haven't learned the system.

Although these fresh faces are young and short on experience, they are armed with great high school highlight tapes and have some of the best opportunities to play. Since nearly all of them are on scholarship, they are very expensive, non-refundable investments—investments that the coaches hope to cash in on immediately. Eagerly, coaches will bump up freshmen and transfers to second, or even, first string based solely on their high school resumes.

When freshman Mike Washington came to the University of Hawai'i after a notable high school career in Pennsylvania, I was the starting X receiver—wide out on the left side—and both Chad Mock and Dave Kaihenui were battling for my spot on the second-string. However, the day Mike was cleared to play, he moved right behind me on the depth chart. This is not unusual. If you are a recruited player, you are treated well. The minute you step off the plane, a plush red carpet is rolled out for you and a beautiful woman greets you with a kiss and a lei. Coach will gingerly walk up to you and—metaphorically, at least—hand you your position on a silver platter. But by the end of his first season, Mike had done nothing on the collegiate level to earn his position, and, more importantly, he had never even had the chance to learn the offense in its entirety.

By the third game, as if destiny were calling, I went down in the second quarter and the coaches threw Mike into the game, expecting the world from him. He lasted two or three games before he was yanked and Chad Mock, a veteran who had had time to adjust to the offense, took over for the remainder of the season. Now Mike's failings had very little to do with his skill and ability, as he was teeming with both. His shortcomings lay on the shoulders of the coaches, with their favoritism and their ability to overlook the 'raw' part of 'raw talent.' What could have been a redshirt year for Mike turned into a three-game season. When coaches decide to gamble and throw an inexperienced kid on the gridiron, they are taking a huge risk. It's a risk that has proven to be very profitable, but it's a risk nonetheless. The key is to let the player, regardless of status, age or experience, earn the position. You wouldn't throw an 8-year-old who's good with a Super Soaker into war with an M16. Let the kid fire off a couple rounds first and see if he's any good at it!

The veterans are the second group of guys who are fighting for No. 1 starter positions. The veterans are likely candidates because they have already learned the ropes and understand what it takes to be a starter. There are three types of veterans: a) bitter and catty b) helpful and confident and c) those who can be both.

The bitter, catty veterans are the ones that feel like the position should already be theirs. This feeling is usually based on their misconception of their own ability or because they were fooled into thinking that seniority had anything to do with playing.

The confident veterans are more like mentors, helping others out whenever they get the chance. They show the new players the tricks of the trade. They welcome a challenge and rely on their own ability to secure the starting job. Their downfall is that they are too concerned with a coach's appraisal. If they feel like the coach noticed their efforts, they feel safe. They think no one will beat them to the starting spot and they'll come off as helpful and cheery. All it takes is a couple of bad blocks or dropped balls and they start doubting their own talent. They will start to feel threatened by everyone and can quickly transform into bitter, catty veterans.

The third group is last year's starters. These players will most likely come out on top for two main reasons. One, they have the experience that is necessary to play high-level football. Two, because they were the starters for a reason, they are the best men for the job. It would be hard for another player—be it a veteran, freshman or transfer—to learn enough about the position in the one-month during fall camp to overtake a previous starter.

The walk-ons are the last group of players who are fighting for the job. I revere them the most. These individuals tend to give the most to the team in terms of pure effort. Come to think of it, walk-ons only really need a few things to make it onto the team—heart, determination, skill and luck. After that, if they can dodge the politics, favoritism and injuries, they're all set. But hold on a minute—that's just what it takes to make it onto the team. They haven't even begun working for their position. This group is given the fewest chances, so time and opportunity are precious for these individuals.

Walking on doesn't just mean working harder than everyone else. It means working harder and being good at what you do. It's not about proving anything to yourself by lifting more or running faster, because if the coaches do not favor you, you are as good as gone. To be a successful walk-on you have to give coaches a reason to let you stay on the team. If you are fast, you must exploit it every chance you get. If you are a hard worker, you make sure it shows. The will of the walk-on is an ironclad force that's tested every day, all day. I call the walk-ons "sleepers," but don't let the name fool you. They get the least sleep of anyone. They are "sleepers" because while everyone is out partying and fooling around, they are watching film and lifting weights. When the team takes it in after practice, they stay out and do cone drills and get on the Jugs football passing machine. They are the "sleepers" because while their teammate are sleeping, they are going for midnight runs or turning on their night lights and studying plays.

Walking on means not only working harder physically but also enduring certain mental discomforts. When the first of the month comes around and the rest of players are picking up their scholarship checks, walk-ons are still attempting to come up with ways to pay for next semester's tuition. While other players talk about buying the latest video game or getting the newest pair of Nike Air Jordans, walk-ons wonder how they can stretch $20 over an entire week. It's hard on the wallet, and the ego. But football is about sacrificing, and walk-ons, by far, have to do it the most. Their journey may be long, but even if they fall short of being the go-to guy, their journey is often the most rewarding.

Jumping, Fighting and Acting, Oh My!

As we all count down the days of summer camp, we look forward to three things—the high dive, pillow fights and the rookie show. The high dive takes place during a practice, usually at the beginning, when Coach calls everyone together and says that if our kicker—this year Dan Kelly—can make a field goal from a certain distance we can end practice and jump into the pool. However, there usually isn't that much pressure, and we go to the pool regardless. But swimming isn't the fun part. What's so exciting about pool day is the 10-meter high dive. Thirty-two feet might not sound too high, but when you climb the platform, and inch up to the edge you're looking down at an extremely scary, intimidating drop. Some of the rookies are balls-to-the-wall and leap off the platform with reckless abandon. The most memorable of these rookies was Pat Olchovy, a wide receiver from New York, who did what was supposed to be a cartwheel off the platform but instead took an awkward plunge that ended with him slamming his stomach and side into the water. The second he hit the entire team cringed in sympathy pain. It looked liked he had broken a rib! But tough New Yorker that he was, or rather tough New Yorker he tried to be, Pat swam to the side, climbed out and strutted around the pool. He had us roaring with laughter. We didn't know what was funnier—his un-athletic jump or his Tony Soprano-like strut!

Another classic jump came from Mike Washington—this time showing literally that he was a small fish in a big pond. Mike plunged into the water and rose to the top kicking and flailing. He had forgotten to mention that he couldn't swim! I think it was Brad Kalilimoku who jumped in after him and pulled him to the edge. Besides earning about three full minutes of laughter, Mike also earned our respect. He showed our Warrior team his fearlessness and fidelity—two characteristics not mandatory to becoming a Warrior, but necessary if we were ever to become a great team.

But, the drop from a 30-foot high dive isn't even the scariest thing about camp—it's the pillow fights! While an unsuspecting player curls helplessly on the ground or in bed, 30 guys ambush him and whack him with pillows. No one is safe from the onslaught, from an innocent veteran bystander to the heavily marked rookie, because from the second one of us grabs that first pillow and begins swinging, the mob mentality spreads like wildfire and everyone's thirsty for some action. The recipient of the beating is better off just curling up and taking it, because if a player runs, he's screwed. Eventually, he'll be caught and the beating will last longer and be a lot more severe. (Pillows can sting, but the shock value is even worse.) The pillow fights are unpredictable, and there's no telling who's going to get it. Most of the beatings happen during summer camp, when all 105 players are sharing the same space. My advice to future players is to sleep with one eye open, stay in the fetal position and take it like a man! These fights are merely a fun way for us to exercise our spirited nature and relieve a dull moment—and to maybe even give a few cushioned blows to someone who's been giving us a bad time on the practice field.

The very end of summer camp means only one thing for us players. And no, it doesn't mean that school is days away. It means it's time for the Rookie Show, when the freshmen and other underclassmen invent creative skits to make everyone laugh. The seniors and coaches are the only ones exempt from participating, but this just means that they will be the main ones parodied and mimicked. Some performances in years past are now legendary. There was quarterback Jeff Rhode, for instance, who did the best Coach Jones impression. He'd walk to the front of the auditorium sporting Jones' trademark faded black sweats and hat. Then, in a dull monotone he'd spout out all of Coach's platitudes, "We have something really special this year." "We have a chance to do something great." "This is the best team I've seen since I've been here." He'd end his monologue with a joke and have the entire auditorium rolling in the aisles!

The coaches always get roasted. It's our only chance to call them on their flaws and follies. Before my senior year, the underclassmen parodied the unsportsmanlike conduct of strength coach Mel deLaura and defensive backs coach Rich Miano. Defensive back Keao Monteilh, who played a convincing Coach Mel, pretended to be stretching the team before practice. Then another player walked up, playing Coach Miano. Defensive back Ryan Keomaka, who was playing Leonard Peters, came over and they all engaged in friendly conversation. "Coach Mel" gave everyone the patented "double-dog" double-fist pound and continued stretching. The best part of the skit came after "Leonard" walked away. Immediately, both "Coach Miano" and "Coach Mel" started talking trash behind his back. The entire room cheered! They had the audacity to put the truth out there and it was hysterical! As always, the closer the parody was to the truth, the funnier it was.

Just because the coaches are teased doesn't mean that the players are safe. In fact, the seniors were the butt of many jokes. One of the funniest skits in 2006 had offensive lineman Tala Esera playing the role of Marissa, our team's equipment manager, and defensive end Ikaika Alama-Francis playing the role of Mel Purcell, another defensive end. They acted out a skit that ended in "Marissa" doing a booty dance on "Mel" to parody their alleged romantic relationship. Nothing and no one was safe during the Rookie Show!

By the end of the show, when all of our stomachs were sore from laughing, we headed out to our dorms, houses and apartments. This fun event was a great way to finish off a rigorous summer camp and begin the regular season. Our first game was just a week away—an away game against the University of Alabama. The only laughing we wanted to be doing a week from now was at the expense of the Crimson Tide. We wanted Alabama to be our first victim.

CHAPTER 2

ALABAMA CRIMSON TIDE

▶ **ON THE FIELD**

Wake-up Calls are a Bitch

"Chad! Wake up. I think we missed the bus!" I yelled.

Chad Mock quickly jumped to his feet and glanced over at the clock, "What do you mean? What time is it?"

"It's 10:35! The bus left at 10:30!" I shouted as I shoved all my belongings into my Nike bag and pulled on my clothes.

"How did we miss the bus? Our alarm never went off! Weren't we supposed to get a wake-up call?" Chad cried.

"I don't know, maybe the bus didn't leave yet. Maybe it's running late. I'll call Ross!" I said.

But both Chad and I knew damn well it wasn't going to be running late. We wouldn't have been so panicked if we were late to a practice or even a meeting, but we were on the verge of missing the bus from Atlanta, Georgia to Tuscaloosa, Alabama—a 200-mile road trip! I dialed Ross Dickerson's phone number, "Riiiiiing...please pick up, Riiiiiing...please pick up, Ross!" I screamed.

"What's up man?" he said.

"Are you on the bus already?" I asked.

"Yeah, why?"

"No reason. Have you guys left already?"

"Yeah, like 10 minutes ago. You aren't here?"

"Not exactly." I told Ross not to tell anyone, that we were going to figure something out. Without a goodbye, I hung up the phone.

"What did Ross say?" Chad asked.

"He said they left 10 minutes ago. Okay, let's calm down, we have to think!"

Chad kept muttering, "The alarm never went off. Why didn't we get a wake-up call?"

While I gathered up all my belongings and thought about what to do next, I tried to remember if we'd gotten a wake-up call. (I've been known to just hang up the phone and go back to sleep.) We packed everything up, and still only half dressed, we raced down to the lobby for any signs of UH football.

To try to reassure Chad and myself that all hope was not lost, I pointed out that the trainers or equipment people could still be around, since they don't take the buses with the rest of the team. I took out my phone and found the number for Brian Wong, one of our head trainers. "Riiiiiing...Wongie! It's Ian. Hey, just wondering, have you guys left already?" I quickly asked him.

"Yeah, we have. Why, did you forget something back at the hotel?"

"Yeah, sort of, kind of. Do you know if the equipment people have left yet?" I asked.

"Yeah, they left, too. What did you forget?"

"Well, Chad and I accidentally woke up late, so we aren't exactly on the bus," I told him.

"Oooooh," he said in a long drawn-out voice. One of those 'Ohs' that mean "you're screwed." I looked down at my phone and Ross was on the other line. I told Wongie not to tell anyone about our situation, and that we would figure something out. I clicked over.

"What's up, Ross?" I asked.

"We barely left, man. Why don't you just call Coach and tell him?" he asked.

"No way! Just don't say anything, okay? We are going to figure this one out!" I quickly hung up.

I looked over at Chad, and as if he and Ross were on the same page, he suggested we should call Coach Jones. I explained to Chad why that would be a bad idea.

"Hell no! You know how pissed he will be if the entire team has to turn around for us. I doubt he'll even turn around—you know how Coach is. We just need to find a way to Alabama. You can call Coach, but I'm not. I'm going to think."

If there was one thing that Coach hated, it was mental errors. Not waking up was a mental error. Not to mention, neither Chad or I were first-string, so any illustration of irresponsibility would not bode well for future playing time. We had to figure this one out on our own.

Then a light bulb turned on over my head. "We can rent a car! I have my credit card. It will be expensive, but shit, I don't care!"

"Don't you have to be older, like 25?" Chad worried.

"I think with a major credit card you can be 21; let's go find out." I said.

We went to the hotel's front desk and asked about local car rental places. The hotel gave us the numbers for Hertz Rent-A-Car, Enterprise and even U-Haul. We sat down on the lobby couches and I dialed away. I was a man on a mission, determined to get a ride to Alabama, regardless of expense.

After the third try, I finally got through to Hertz. I explained my urgent situation and the representative assured me a car by 3 p.m. This being the only ounce of hope we had, I was greatly relieved. Then I looked at my phone and was reminded it was only 10:55 a.m.! Three p.m. meant that Chad and I would miss practice, dinner, meetings and film. And, it definitely meant that we would have no chance to play. It was hopeless.

As I was pleading with Hertz and listening to Chad still trying to figure out why we didn't get a wake-up call, Wongie called. I gave the Hertz dealer a quick bye, and I clicked over. "Please tell me something good, Wongie!"

"Eric (the head trainer) just talked to (athletic director) Herman Frazier and found out that he hasn't left for Alabama yet," Wongie said.

"Are you serious? Can I get his number? Do you know if he's leaving today or anytime soon?"

"I just talked to him and he said that he's in the computer lab at the hotel," Wongie said.

"Holy shit, Wongie, thanks! I'll call you back," I said and hung up the phone. I yelled to Chad that Herman Frazier was in the hotel and that we needed to find the computer lab.

Chad exclaimed, "I saw computers over there!" He pointed down a hallway to the right of the concierge. We both scrambled to the computer lab where we found our savior typing away.

"Hey, Mr. Frazier," Chad said ever so calmly, as if we both weren't on the verge of cardiac arrest. "Do you have any room in your car?"

He laughed and told us he heard what happened. He said, "I'm not going to leave for another 20 minutes or so, and it might be a squeeze, but we can take you."

"Yes, thank you so much," Chad said.

I chimed in, "Yes, thank you so much. We're really sorry. We missed our alarm and the wake-up call, and we were doing everything to find a ride."

Mr. Frazier then asked, "Did you call Coach and tell him?"

"No! I mean, no. I don't want him to know anything about this. Just as long as we get there in time for practice, we're fine," I reassured Mr. Frazier.

Why was everyone so hell-bent on telling Coach Jones? It wasn't like he would do anything to help the situation. Chad and I returned to the lobby and sat down on the couches, out of breath and relieved. Well, semi-relieved because if we were going to make it to the walk-through practice at Alabama's stadium we still needed Mr. Frazier to leave soon.

After a long, cramped trip in Mr. Frazier's car we arrived in Tuscaloosa. By the time we set foot into our new hotel, everyone knew about our panicky predicament. But since we didn't miss anything, the coaches really didn't care. In fact, it was the ongoing joke for the entire season. Whenever we showed up for anything we were teased, "Glad you could make it" or "Thanks for joining us!"

Game Strategy:
Beat a big-name team in a big-time conference.

Bryant-Denny Stadium—a crowd of nearly 100,000. It was the biggest stadium most of us had played in and the crowd was the loudest we'd ever heard. The seats were filled with a rowdy, red-and-white mob that wanted just one thing—to see us taro-pickin' heathens strung up from the rafters. We were in hostile territory. The stadium was unfamiliar and the fans were all rooting against us. But it didn't matter; the game was the same. The field was still 100 yards from goal line to goal line; we still had to battle against 11 men, and we still had to play the game of football at the highest level. Just another day at the office. With the roar of the crowd, we went on a silent count. That meant that Colt Brennan wouldn't use a cadence or shout out, "Set, go!" We waited for Samson Satele to hike the ball. For this to work we all had to be on the same page—it shouldn't be a problem—we practiced all summer that way.

We won the toss, which was great. We loved receiving the ball first. Kenny Patton and Ross Dickerson were back to return the kickoff. Alabama's kicker raised his hand, the whistle blew and boom—our season was officially underway. Ross caught the ball and charged forward 48 yards. It was a great way to open the game. The offense marched out on the field and broke from the huddle. The first play was a sideline pass to Ross, who made a diving grab to haul it in. We wanted to score first to keep the pressure off of the defense. Our starting running back, Nate Ilaoa, had a couple of good runs and Colt made some quick throws to our premier wide receiver, Davone Bess. We slowly gained yards, inch by inch. Alabama stopped us on third and four, so we had to settle for a field goal. Daniel Kelly booted a 42-yarder. It was good to know that our kicker could make those kinds of kicks. The offense returned to the sideline, and you could tell by the look in their eyes they weren't satisfied. We hated field goals. Those three points reminded us how we failed to go a measly 10 more yards for a first down.

Now it was time for our defense to play. We held our breath; defense was often our weak link. Alabama opened up with the run. We expected that since that was the Crimson Tide's MO. We stood on the sideline and watched Alabama run its way down the field. However, it wasn't their running that concerned us most—it was their passing game. We knew we could eventually stop the ground game, but we wanted to see how we fared against the air attack.

The ball was snapped, and their quarterback dropped back and looked downfield. We all shouted "Pass!" to alert our defense. The QB lobbed a jump ball down the sideline and the receiver made the catch over our defensive backs. There was good and bad news about that play. The good news was that Alabama's quarterback didn't have great arm strength or accuracy. The bad news was that he didn't need it when his tall receivers could win most any 50/50 jump balls over our cornerbacks.

On that drive, Alabama didn't pass much. And, when they ran, we swarmed to the ball, making late tackles four to five yards downfield. However, our defense stuck together and the Tide settled for a field goal.

Our ensuing offensive drive consisted of a personal foul, a dropped pass and a punt. It was far less successful than we had hoped, especially since our wide receiver coach Ron Lee had predicted that we'd need 30 points to win the game. The only thing positive that came out of the drive was that Nate looked fast and healthy. Plagued with injuries since arriving at UH, Nate was a killer weapon when he was intact. With him healthy, our one-dimensional offense became 2D. This was a plus since Davone had already dropped two balls in the game and the other receivers weren't doing much better. If we were playing poorly because of first-game jitters, we needed to get over it in a hurry.

Our defense ran out on the field again and tried desperately to stop the surging Crimson Tide. They pounded the ball right down our throats. They didn't pass the ball the entire series, and in a matter of minutes, they were back up on the board, ahead 10-3.

The rest of the first half showed no offensive improvements. We didn't get first downs, we fumbled the ball, and to top it off, we gave up a safety when the ball went right through punter Kurt Milne's hands and out the back of the end zone.

We went in at halftime disappointed and angry. We needed to change our game strategy and our intensity. We played like we didn't deserve to be there—we were playing like the underdogs we were. We regrouped and marched back out onto the field with a different demeanor. Our defense held the Tide to only 10 points the entire second half. We held one of the best running backs in the nation, Kenneth Darby, to just 25 yards on 16 carries. And when it was crunch time in the fourth quarter, the defense came up with huge stops to give our offense chances to score.

Our offense also came out of halftime with a lot more fire. Regan Mauia, our second-string running back, recorded our first touchdown of the season on a 17-yard pass, proving to Alabama and his fellow Warriors that he could not only block, but he could also run when we needed him to. His touchdown was followed by another touchdown catch in the fourth quarter by one of our slot receivers, Ryan Grice-

Mullins, for 32 yards. However, our efforts on offense were too little and came too late. With one second left and down by 8, our hopes were crushed by a game-ending interception. We left the field angry and frustrated. We had lost to a mediocre team, 25-17.

In the locker room some of the seniors spoke out. They said we should all hold our heads up high—that we fought together as a team. They said we played our hearts out. I hated this complacent attitude, especially after a loss. The fact is, we were not the victors, nor did we play our hardest. The only thing we learned was that the flavor of failure tasted like shit. Although I didn't agree with the "hold your head up high" speeches or "we did our best" comments, I did notice something else while I watched our team play and lose. It was subtle and hard to decipher among the turnovers, mishaps and lost opportunities, but it was there—a sparkle.

It's like two kids in a fist fight. The younger, weaker kid puts up a good fight, but by the end of it he lays bloodied and beaten in the dirt. The older kid kicks him one last time for good measure and walks away with his hands held high in victory. Now, if you look real hard, as it happens within a blink of an eye, you'd see the beaten and bruised kid look up and stare straight at the bully, and there you'd see that that kid isn't broken at all. You'd see revenge, hope, anger and power creep out from inside and sparkle in his eye. The loss brought out something special. That kid—our team—had a lot more fight left in us. We just needed something to awaken our sleeping giant. This had simply been our first wake-up call.

▶ OFF THE RECORD

A Dark Lesson in Selflessness

"Character is what you are in the dark." —Dwight L. Moody

All around the locker room and academic center there were quotes posted—some inspiring, some educational and others insightful. The one above was posted right before the entrance to the training room. "Character is what you are in the dark." I passed by it every day, pondered its meaning, and then dismissed it as just another clever saying. It's hard to take a bunch of words seriously when you've yet to apply them to your own life. But with our season opener behind us, I now felt like I was in the dark. I had been a starter last year and had also had a great spring training, yet I found myself second in line to Ross Dickerson for my position. I had sat out nearly the entire Alabama game, only getting a rep or two in the 3rd and 4th quarters.

But when I refer to character and darkness in this case, I'm not talking about myself. What happened in the dark—never revealed in a press conference or a team meeting—took place after that game, when we returned to Hawai'i. Ironically, I learned about someone's character "in the dark" on a sunny Monday morning. After our weekly running, when Ross and I were walking back to the locker room, he said to me, "Next game, you can start."

At first I was confused. I don't think I really understood what he said. "What?" I asked.

"You can start next game," he repeated.

It took me a couple seconds to fully grasp what he was saying. Most anyone else might have said, "Yes!" with no questions asked.

But being the analytical person that I am, I slowly became irritated and thought, *He doesn't have the power to give me the position.* I was going to take it in my own right.

"You've earned it," Ross said. "You've worked so hard. It's not fair if you don't play."

Surprised and annoyed, I retorted, "Thanks, but if I do start, I want Coach to make that decision, not you."

"Well, you know, I'm not going to slow down or stop working hard," he said.

"I know, and neither am I," I answered.

I went into the locker room and tried to figure out what just happened. I realized that I was angry because although I was content in being a back-up, I in no way liked being reminded by the starter that I was second-string. I didn't want to be reminded that he had the position over me. I couldn't have imagined saying yes to his offer. I prefer the satisfaction of earning things. As I'd promised him at the end of the conversation, I still planned on earning and taking the starting job.

It took me a while to realize what Ross had done. I tried to figure out what he had to gain by coming to me with this far-fetched proposal. I sat and thought long and hard on the locker room bench. After my anger subsided, it hit me. I realized that Ross had come to me without tricks, conditions or gimmicks behind his actions. He was being selfless. He wanted to see me start because he knew how hard I had worked in the off-season and he also knew that I, too, could get the job done. He didn't approach me because he was injured or sick of the game. He approached me as a teammate out of selflessness and sincerity.

I thought back to earlier in the summer when Coach first moved me from X receiver to Z receiver. I welcomed the change because I knew I'd have to battle it out with Ross. I'd have to compete with a true player of the game, a player with no ego, one who's all work and determination. Those Ross types only make you better. And now Ross had brought selflessness into the equation. A characteristic that can be highly contagious and one that any great team possesses. That day, Ross spread the contagious bug of selflessness to me and in return earned my respect— an honor I reserved only for those with crowning integrity. Whether he knew it or not, he had provided the foundation for the quality that would characterize our team for the remainder of the season.

▶ IN THE LOCKER ROOM

On the starting job ...

"Man, I'd never give up my spot. Someone would have to take it from me. My spot is something I work for every damn day. No sense in being reckless with something like that. Shit, selflessness is good and all, but I think I'm the only man that can get the job done at the highest level. I'm staying in until Coach pulls me out."

"Only some of the players don't have to work hard for their jobs. It's either because they're naturally gifted or because the coaches like them. Either way, you have to perform come game day, or they'll find someone else. You work so hard to be a starter, so giving it away doesn't make all that much sense."

"If I knew I wasn't performing the way I should be, then maybe I'd call in my backup. But still yet, even if I didn't think I was doing the job, I'd probably stay in there and try to make up for it. I don't think I could tell someone else to start the following game."

On Ross Dickerson...

"The first thing that comes to mind when I think of Ross is his runs. He's not afraid to lower his head and just run into people. That gets the crowd and the rest of the team going. It's good for the game."

"He'll play with you, joke with you and drink with you. He's a team player for real. And I've never heard him complain. He's one of those guys that just gets the job done."

CHAPTER 3

UNLV RUNNIN' REBELS

▶ **ON THE FIELD**

No One Likes a Rebel

After our close loss to Alabama and a bye week to help us shake it, we turned our attention toward the University of Nevada–Las Vegas Runnin' Rebels. On film UNLV was nothing special, but we kept in mind that it had been a while since we'd had a W. We prayed we still knew what that stood for.

It was our home opener at good ol' Aloha Stadium. We were all a little anxious to play at home for our friends and family. We were minutes away from kickoff. The artificial smoke was cued, the band played our music and we ran out of the tunnel onto the field. It was not as thrilling as it should have been. We saw more empty seats than full ones. It was not a great turnout, especially for our first home game. We understood that many people are fair-weather fans. We had to get the job done if we wanted to see better crowds.

To our surprise, our captain and starting free safety, Leonard Peters, was playing despite his rib cartilage damage. Nothing was going to hold us back from getting this much-needed win, and Leonard led by example. That wasn't the only good news, for this game, Ross and I were switching in and out. No more playing second string. Coach Jones said in the film room after the Alabama game that the Xs and Zs were going to rotate. (Ross and I were Zs—right-side wide receivers—while Chad and Jason Rivers were Xs, wide receivers who lined up at far left.)

Game Strategy:
Can we please get a W?

With the flip of the coin, the game was underway. We won the toss and elected to receive. We needed to score early to avoid becoming a second-half team—a team that needed pressure to perform. We also needed to work on finishing our drives. We were a good open-field team, but in the red zone our offense was far less productive. Our opening drive was throw-and-catch. Colt read the defense and we made easy catches and simple runs. We reached the end zone in no time. It only took two minutes and six plays for the referee to throw up his hands, signaling our first at-home touchdown.

Dan Kelly kicked off to UNLV's go-to guy, Eric Wright, who mustered up a decent return. Our defense read the first play perfectly—we swarmed, loss of two yards. Second play, not much more for UNLV. On third down, UNLV was going to throw the ball. The offense and I got up on our feet to watch. The ball was snapped, and we had the quarterback in the backfield, but he slipped away and heaved the ball 30 yards for a completion—not again! Our secondary needed to step it up if we were going to run away with this game.

As if answering our sideline prayers, the secondary—along with the rest of the defense—did come up big. They held UNLV scoreless for the entire half. That night we made it look easy. Colt went nine for nine for 106 yards and two touchdowns on the first two drives of the game. I also recorded my first catch of the season. It came in the third drive—a quick out. I dove for the ball, but I'm not sure if the dive was completely necessary. Sometimes you dive so you can focus better on the ball, letting your feet and body go so that your eyes and mind can fully concentrate on the spiraling pigskin coming your way. The first catch of the season is always a tricky one. You're not sure if your nerves will get the best of you. But when you do catch it, you remind yourself that you've been here before and you're in control—all you have to do is play.

I was all smiles for the rest of the game, as were all our players. UNLV wasn't anything special. The slot receivers had a good game. Ryan had seven catches for 111 yards and one touchdown, while Davone amassed 124 yards and one touchdown off of 10 catches. And let's not forget our cartilage-damaged captain, Leonard, who had a 33-yard interception return. The final score was 42-13, Hawai'i's first win!

▶ **OFF THE RECORD**

Hawai'i's Rebel with a Cause

In the UNLV game, we receivers faced one of the best cornerbacks we'd see all season. Eric Wright started at the University of Southern California, then for personal reasons transferred to Nevada–Las Vegas. Both Ross and I ran against him. He was athletic, quick, fleet-footed and had the potential to be a great cover-corner. He ran stride for stride with both of us, which I promise is hard to do. But it wasn't his athleticism that I noticed first; it was his attitude, his playing demeanor. Usually from the first play you can tell how tough a defender is going to be. During your first pass play, you feel him out for his speed. You run your absolute fastest to see if he can hang. Then on the first run play, when you have to block him, you feel him out to see if you're stronger than he is. You try to estimate his tendencies, his strengths and weaknesses, then try to prey on the latter. Yet the biggest weakness anyone can hope to find in an opponent is not strength, speed or even ability—it's heart.

A player who lacks heart is by far the easiest opponent. And these players are what I like to call "I-guys," because they are mostly concerned about themselves. Don't get me wrong—they are usually superior athletes, because I-guys who can't play worth a lick don't make it as far as NCAA Division 1 football. And players with little ability and skill need to rely on their heart and work ethic to make it. So by default, almost all I-guys are gifted athletes. And, with enough skill, they can make it extremely far in athletics.

You could tell that Wright was strictly an I-guy. The kind of guy that you can imagine saying, "I had my man covered, so I did my job," "I'm not going to make that tackle, that's your responsibility," or "I'm not running over there, I might get tired." Wright didn't try; there was no effort behind his play. If Ross or I knew the play was going to the other side, then we knew we could take a play off if we wanted. There was no chance that our I-guy would make the effort. I saw this attitude in a lot of star players. And I'm not deliberately picking on Mr. Wright. I gave him the benefit of the doubt and said it could have been an off day for him. However, when you only play 12 games in a season, you should make sure that one of your off days doesn't fall on a Saturday in autumn.

I-guys may have no heart, but what they lack in heart, they make up for with their big mouths! They are typically the biggest talkers on the field. They'll let you know that they banged out your momma last night and tell you how bad she was. They'll constantly remind you that they own you and are your daddy. They'll be sure to tell you that you're slow, ugly and have no hands. And they will be the first ones to stroke their own egos and point out that you are going against the No. 1 corner, defensive back, linebacker, lineman, whatever, in the nation. I-guys trash-talk!

Trash talking is one of the most fascinating parts of football. What makes football a haven for this kind of dialogue is the closeness of opponents. More or less, for an entire game any given player, no matter his position, is going against the same opposing player time and time again. One of two things can happen: a) the players form a mutual respect for one another or b) the players grow to hate one another. But regardless of the relationship, trash-talking will occur.

Ryan Grice-Mullins said, "If you can trash-talk to your opponent and he starts to believe it, then you're already in his head. You've got that slight advantage over him."

Trash talking isn't only words. It's high stepping in the end zone, it's hand gestures and it's touchdown dances—it's showboating. Today, showboating is applauded. Everyone sits up to watch the Cincinnati Bengals' Chad Johnson's new and unique touchdown celebrations. Who doesn't remember his "Riverdance" after scoring against a deflated Cleveland Browns team? These dances, these taunts are synonymous with football—Merton Hanks of the 49ers and Seahawks and his funky chicken, or Dallas' Terrell Owens and the Sharpie in his sock. And they're not all by individuals. There are more choreographed team celebrations, such as the Atlanta Falcons' "Dirty Bird," the St. Louis Rams' "Bob and Weave" or maybe what paved the way for all the others—the Washington Redskins' "Fun Bunch High-five."

However, I-guys don't stop at vulgar vernacular and end zone capers. The ultimate sign of an I-guy is the third-person reference. When they are alluding to themselves, instead of saying 'I' or 'me,' they use their own name. For instance, if I write, "Ian scored 10 touchdowns this season" or "Ian likes to help the children," no matter how I use the third person, whether I'm bragging or stating simple facts, I come off as smug and uppity.

I was a child the first time I heard the third-person used in football. It was in the movie "Necessary Roughness," when Andre Krimm, played by Sinbad, says to his coach, "Andre does not eat raw meat. 'Cause Andre is a vegetarian." But it's not just in the movies where we see these third-person references. Terrell Owens refers to himself as "T.O." in interviews and Chad Johnson told reporters he doesn't go by Chad or even No. 85, but by "Ocho-Cinco." Having nicknames is one thing, but creating them yourself and referring to yourself by them seems a little extreme. But once again, let me take T.O., Ocho-Cinco and even Mr. Wright off of the hot seat. The media can blow things way out of proportion, and I'll admit that I don't really know these players. I only know what I see or what I hear.

A certain Hawai'i Warrior fits the profile of an I-guy. He calls himself the "The Kid" or "O-1-N-A" (Only One in America), but you might be more used to hearing his given name, Ryan Grice-Mullins.

Ryan was by far the biggest showboat on our team. He was the quickest to get up after being tackled just so he could bark back at an opponent, letting him know that his tackle wasn't shit. He was the first to cross the end zone, unbuckle his chinstrap and celebrate. In 2005, it was the synchronized, vertical leap with Davone, while in 2006 Ryan did more of a high-step, high-knee, solo celebration. But that was just the tip of the iceberg. Ryan wasn't just all flash on game day. He saved most of it for the other six days of the week—and it started with his attire. When most of us were half asleep at 6 a.m., slowly dressing ourselves for practice, he would match from head to toe. He was usually adorned all in white, but he's been known to call a fashion audible or two on muddy days. Needless to say, he had the most flair on the team, and the most paraphernalia, including matching wristbands, socks, shoelaces and backpack.

If all that jazz didn't make him a bona fide member of the I-guy team then his third-person speech could have made him the founder. I mean, he called himself the "The Kid" or "O-1," which was an abbreviated version for "O-1-N-A." And if he wasn't out of breath with all that said, he'd continue, "The kid, O-1, from the IE all day every day. West coastin' all day, gotta represent the west 'cause the west is the best." What a mouthful! So when all was said and done, it seemed that Ryan Grice-Mullins was just another showboating, trash-talking, dance-doing I-guy. Which would've been totally true, if I hadn't gotten to know him.

While showboating, taunting and trash-talking can often separate a player from his team, it had the exact opposite effect for Ryan and our Warriors. He added the spice that every team should have. After a long practice, when we were tired and all we could think about was skipping a couple classes to take a nap, he'd crack everyone up when he'd juke out a defender then toss him the ball, as if saying "Oh, you wanted this? Here you go." Or, after a long meeting in the film room, Ryan made us laugh when he'd ask Coach to rewind the tape so he could watch his touchdown celebration—this time maybe in slow motion. All in all, it was humorous because it was harmless. But his cockiness, his I-guy-like qualities lacked the final component to make him a full-blooded I-guy—selfishness. On the field he was not afraid to lay down a block for any one of us. He was not too scared to go across the middle if we needed a first down. He was in it to win it, but to win it as part of a team. Ryan's cockiness was reflected in his words, not in his disposition.

However, admiration for a football player should never begin on the football field. Admiration for Ryan began far away from the cleats and pigskin. It started at 4 a.m., outside on a track, in the pouring rain. While walking around a track from dawn to dusk may seem daft to some, to others like Ryan, the reasons are clear. For example, the UH Relay for Life raised money and awareness for cancer research. The Student Athletic Advisory Committee, run by UH athletes, hosted a cancer walk. The previous two rainy years tested the will of the participants. The event wasn't mandatory, and it was held on a Friday night, when many college kids were out partying. But Ryan sat and walked through the rain for hours, listening to the cancer survivors and their family members tell their heartbreaking tales. He walked several laps around the puddled track because, although physically the laps were effortless, it meant more to him than any night out clubbing and dancing in Waikiki.

But don't get me wrong. Ryan partied with the best of us—when the time and occasion were right. I've seen him acting wild on the dance floor several times. Those memories may fade but I'll always remember Ryan dancing the funky chicken and electric slide at the Foster Care Holiday Party. I asked Ryan if he could go with me to the party because I knew he would say yes. We spent the day signing autographs and dancing with the children at the party. It was a little embarrassing trying to relearn the macarena, whose death I had prayed for back in the '90s. As I tried to figure out which went first, the hands to the hip or to the head, I looked over and saw Ryan not missing a beat. He was totally absorbed in his own world of music and children.

Our Warrior team was immersed, and even defined, by its different characters—each with their own personality, attitude and culture. I don't doubt, in fact I know, that there were I-guys on our team. But when I looked at our starting slot receiver from Rialto, California, he was no I-guy—just one of our most colorful characters. And, we wouldn't have wanted it any other way.

▶ IN THE LOCKER ROOM
with Ryan Grice-Mullins

On trash-talking ...

"Trash-talking is a big part of football. Most people don't understand it unless they are a football player, or unless they are on the field. A lot of people think it's bad for the game, but I think it's good. Once you're off the field, you can be cool with your opponent."

On his many nicknames ...

"My first nickname was in high school, they called me "guns." And a lot of people think it's "big guns" and they say, "He ain't big, he ain't buff, he ain't strong. What people don't really know is that they call me big guns because big guns make big plays and add big points at big games. Next is 'O1NA,' which stands for "Only One in America." The reason for that is because I'm the only person that has the name Grice-Mullins. My mom doesn't, I don't have any brothers and I'm the only child. And my dad's name isn't Grice-Mullins; I'm the only one. That's why I'm "O1NA." A lot of people think it's my number, but it's not. I've never been No. 1 till I got here. And IE is Inland Empire, that's where I'm from, ya feel me, represent the IE all day every day."

On giving back ...

"I appreciate being in the position that I'm in. A lot of guys don't get a chance to play college ball. A lot of kids dream of playing college ball, and they look up to us. Just to see it in their faces, when you go back to help a little kid, they are shocked to look at you. To them you're someone amazing. For kids to look up to you like that, it's the best. Being in our position gives us the chance to give something back."

CHAPTER 4

BOISE STATE BRONCOS

▶ **ON THE FIELD**

Trying to Saddle the Broncos

It was bad enough that football players are stereotyped as jocks, dimwitted and ill mannered. But even in the world of college football, other teams saw our Hawai'i team as a bunch of wild, tattooed, ungroomed, reckless thugs. We threw punches first, they said, and asked questions later. Just ask Cincinnati, Houston or San Jose State. So how does a team earn respect, win a game and change a stereotype all in one night? It's impossible, but we tried our darndest.

Game Strategy:
No turnovers!

September 23rd, that was the day that would decide who was going to be WAC champions. If we beat Boise State, which was on a 21-0 winning streak, we could win the rest of our games. Boise felt the same about beating us. They were a good team—not great, but solid. They had excellent special teams and they were good at forcing turnovers. We had better athletes, but we still weren't altogether confident about playing away games. The last time we'd seen Boise on its blue field, the so-called "Smurf turf," we had lost on national TV by an embarrassing 69-3! We had a chip on our collective shoulder, and we wanted to prove that we weren't that team of the past. On our opening drive Coach decided to hail the ball out to Jason Rivers. Jason had a clean release; he quickly lost his defender. Colt dropped back in the pocket, he had the protection, and he heaved the ball deep down the field to a wide-open

Jason! It hit his hands and dropped straight through his arms! It was the first of many missed opportunities that day.

We failed to hit extra points. One botched attempt was even blocked by Boise State and then returned 90-plus yards for a two-point play. Davone ran a great route, snagged the ball from the air and made several defenders miss—only to get stripped and turn over the ball. Colt scrambled to make something happen, and then he fumbled. We knew the game was about turnovers, yet we turned the ball over time and time again. By the end of the game all we could do was to pray to get lucky, for some anomaly to occur so we could squeak out a victory. No such thing happened. We went home losers, with a 1-2 record on the season.

"I hate Boise. I hate their team with a passion," Jason said afterwards. "They've beat us up for the last couple years, so I really wanted to win this game more than any of other ones."

▶ OFF THE RECORD

Turning Negatives into Positives

How do you wash away such a loss? How does a team get over the idea that we now had to rely on other teams to beat Boise State so we could at least share the WAC title? And most important, how do we beat the bad rap that we can't win on the road, when we just suffered two straight losses away? The fact is, you don't wash it away. You simply learn from it. You can't do anything about the past; it happened and there is no way of going back to change it. Tell yourself that and pray that you'll believe it. The only thing you can correct is your attitude toward the future.

That night we did nothing to reassure our fans or anyone else watching the game that we could be a successful away team. It sounds odd but the loss was exactly what we needed. The defeat helped us change from that young kid beaten on the ground to an enraged Warrior football team.

Jason Rivers led the charge. The same Jason who dropped the opening, potentially game-changing, ball. Jason was one of the first guys to realize that we needed to play at a higher tempo in order to change people's minds about us. For the remainder of the Boise game, Jason called on his dropped ball as an incentive to do better. Some find it easier than others, but a player needs to go into each play as if it's its own game. You can't think about past plays. Negativity from prior plays can't lapse into the present. You make something good out of something bad. You turn a dropped ball into six catches for 81 yards and three touchdowns. And above all, you know that you can never be fully broken. Like Jason, our team would not give up, not until the last whistle blew.

Escaping Stereotypes

On the field, through brawn and determination, was where we tried to change preconceived notions about our team. But that wasn't the only place we battled stereotypes. Off the field, at home and at school, we were seen as mindless, cocky, arrogant jocks. The word "jock" alone evokes an image of a dim-witted, muscle-bound moron. These off-the-field stereotypes were the hardest to break because we live with them every second, hour and day. Every day, people condemned us, putting us into little boxes labeled "Dumb," "Typical" or "Womanizer." These labels take me back to the week before we left to play Boise State, when I overheard a conversation as I dug into a Chalupa Supreme at our on-campus Taco Bell.

Girl #1: "Did you just see who walked by? Jason Rivers! How dumb is he, getting kicked out of school when he was on a full ride."

Boy: "I knew him in high school. Probably thinks he's the shit. Guaranteed if he didn't have his boys around he'd catch lickin's."

Girl #2: "Seriously, he tried hitting on me one time, with that arrogant swagger and his head all high in the air, but I wasn't having it."

Girl #1: "You go, sista!"

Was Jason dumb, cocky, arrogant and a womanizer? To be perfectly honest, a lot of us fit into these categories, myself included. I have been cocky and arrogant and I have womanized. I've had my moments of stupidity, and at times I think with my libido instead of my brain.

But let's play devil's advocate and take a closer look at Jason, who will serve as our quintessential UH football player. I guess you could say that Jason failing out of school was pretty dumb. Maybe he just didn't have what it took to be college material. Academia was just not his thing. Or maybe he was just whisked through St. Louis School because he was an exceptional athlete. Who knows the reason? All I know is what goes through the mind of a receiver like Jason on any given day. Let me paint you a picture. It's game day and the offense has the ball. In the huddle, Colt says, "Trips right, 781 special X choice."

Jason runs from the huddle and has some thinking to do:

Trips right, 781 special X choice. X choice, choice splits, the ball is in the left hash so I'm a yard inside the numbers. Okay, scan the defense. The safety is kicking down, check four across man, warn the offense. Check alert, check alert! I have a three-step break if they keep the blitz on. Get ready to run. Colt's about to snap it. Wait, the safety is dropping off. It's not a blitz! What's my corner doing? Playing off and inside. Are they showing cover 3 or man now? Go! On my seventh step I have to break the post or out, 1-3-5, my man is still high and on top of me, No. 7! Break the out! Make it smooth, come downhill, the ball's in the air, keep my eyes on it, make sure I get the first down, drag the foot. Good, next play. Get back to the huddle.

Anyone who can do all that thinking in four seconds while winded in a dead sprint against someone who wants nothing but to physically harm him, is unquestionably an above-average thinker. Granted, football smarts and academic smarts may have limited correlation. But football players are trained to think fast. We are trained to make split-second decisions. The most beautiful part is that once you're trained, your body makes the decisions for you. The thinking and the playing become one. It all becomes second nature.

Most college students, of course, pursue studies that they hope will pay off later in life. In the same way, most football players will try to apply the lessons of the game to life after college. Not all of us make a successful career out of our sport, but there is no sense in giving up the dream before we have the chance to prove ourselves in it—or before our sport proves to us it doesn't want or need us. One benefit of college athletics is that we are more or less forced to graduate, or at least complete a large percentage of our degree by the time our college career is over. Typically, our degree is our backup plan and luckily it comes by default.

Without a doubt, it wasn't a smart move when Jason lost his scholarship, was temporarily suspended from school and missed an entire season of football. But the dumbest thing he could have done would have been to give up. After Jason left the team and UH there were few choices for him. Coach couldn't put him back in the game of life and make sure he redeemed himself. The only way he could right his wrong was on his own. Making mistakes and being "dumb" is expected. After all, to err is human. But forging your own path while learning from your mistakes is what I'd consider the highest form of intelligence.

"I didn't care about school at all the first couple years," Jason told me. "I did just enough to get by. But when I lost it all, it was like my legs got cut from under me. Football is my life. So I needed to come back, and I also knew the school work wasn't that hard." The semester he returned to school, he got a 3.2.

So maybe now you see a different side of Jason, at least as far as his decision-making is concerned, but that doesn't negate the fact that he walked around with an inflated ego. As the guy at Taco Bell put it, "He probably thinks he's the shit." Around campus we all felt bigger than usual. It had a lot to do with the fact that we were bigger than usual. We were among the biggest because we lifted weights. And we lifted weights because that was our job. However, there is a difference between being big and acting big, and it wasn't difficult to distinguish. The reason we acted big is because we had confidence. Where does this confidence come from? In part, it came from knowing we had 100 of our teammates and friends around us at all times. I'd bet that if UH had a math team that was 100 people deep and they did nothing but math equations, problem solving and fallacy findings for the better half of their day, they would not only walk around taller, but their shared experience would have them walking more confidently. I'd go as far as saying that some of them would actually think that they're better than the average Joe. This attitude is not a football mentality but a human one.

Our confidence also came from being in top shape, which can also inspire feelings of superiority. We trained harder than average individuals. We had to because our livelihoods are on the line. We were faster and stronger, so physically we felt superior. Actually posturing this superiority was a matter of ego, of course. It was our choice whether to avoid it or let it completely envelope us.

So Girl #2 said that Jason "tried hitting on me one time, with that arrogant swagger and his head all high in the air." Listen here, Girl #2, what is hitting on you but a little charm? And what is charm but simply a way of talking? So his words were smooth and his attitude dismissive? I admire that. More than likely, the only words that left his lips were, "Hey, how are you?"

It is preconceived notions that often contribute to negative stereotypes. When a football player says "Hi" to a pretty girl, he's hitting on her. A lot of girls throw up walls and wave red flags. But take a non-player and put him in the same situation, and those same girls might be more willing to have a conversation, more willing to open up.

Jason argues, "We just do what we do and people are going to assume things about us anyway, so it doesn't matter to me."

Many of the players were smooth talkers. We knew what to say and when to say it. Yet, there was really nothing deceptive about it. It was just having that confidence that's the key component to doing anything with relative ease. With confidence behind our words, we weren't going to stutter and stumble like some babbling rookie. Instead, we flattered and finessed like seasoned pros, because we weren't afraid to come right out and say, "Nice legs," or "Love the way your eyes look with that shirt."

Some might call that arrogance. But I think many players felt this is something they earned. We were Warriors, after all, who returned home every Monday during football season, back to our campus. The same campus we woke up to at the crack of dawn to do battle every day on the practice field. The same campus we left 13 days a year to go to war against unbending odds. We had that Warrior swagger because we believed that football was life. Football was our life. So please excuse Jason and the rest of us for the swagger in our step that might seem excessive. The fact is, we would never put our heads down, partly because by the end of the day, we knew we had worked harder than most people do in a week.

▶ IN THE LOCKER ROOM

"We are stereotyped all the time. It would be different if it was just a handful of us being stereotyped, but there are more than 100 of us. We travel in numbers and we all carry the same stereotype. So it doesn't affect us. Besides, no one has the balls to say anything to us anyway. And most likely those people are just jealous. They want what we got—fame."

"Man, when it comes to girls stereotyping us, it doesn't even matter. If someone is going to judge me without meeting me then screw it. One time I walked up to a girl and tried to spit game, and she said that she had heard about us football players and that she wasn't having it. Right there just shows how ignorant people are—she ain't worth talking to anyways. So I just told her what I heard about blondes—they're all chicken heads."

"Sometimes it's the best thing when teachers and other students stereotype you, because they expect you to be some mindless jock. But if you show even an ounce of intelligence or thought then you're looked at as an exception. You're even looked up to as having both brains and brawn. It's not bad being a smart jock and an athletic student. You got the best of both worlds."

XXXXXXXXXXXXXXXXXXXXX
CHAPTER 5

EASTERN ILLINOIS PANTHERS

▶ ON THE FIELD

Opportunity Doesn't Just Knock

It wasn't easy losing to a Division 1-AA team. But we'd done it before so we didn't take the game against Eastern Illinois lightly. Plus they weren't a conference team so the chances of a rematch were slim to none. In this game, we wanted to jump ahead early and show the Panthers that they didn't deserve to play with us. With Ryan Grice-Mullins injured the week before in Boise, Coach Jones made some personnel changes. Aaron "Yoda" Bain was Ryan's backup but I knew there was a chance that Coach would send Ross over to do the job. (Ross had started as a slot receiver when he first arrived at UH so he would be more comfortable with the position change.) I prayed for this to happen because I knew it would give me the chance to start, not to mention it would put the best receivers across the line.

When Tuesday morning came around and Ross was at slot, it was difficult to contain my happiness. The change also gave Chad Mock the ability to switch back and forth at Z and X, so if Coach decided to rotate or if Jason or I were tired, Chad would back us up.

Every week was like an audition. When it was game time you had to play your best because there was always someone waiting backstage who wanted your spot. Given the opportunity to start meant I was try-ing out for the starting job for the rest of the season. I was no longer fighting to get the job—I was fighting to keep it. Ross was in the same boat. He knew that Ryan was only going to be out for so long, so he had to perform to the best of his ability if he wanted to keep his starting job. That week both Ross and I took the time to run extra after practice because a full game with no rotating takes it out of you. The last thing we wanted was to run up the score on the Panthers and then not be able to perform to the best of our ability. Hell, this was a chance to up our stats, too. So as Forrest Gump would say, "we were runnin'," every day for what seemed like all day to make sure we were the best fit for the job.

Game Strategy:
Don't make it close!

We won the toss and elected to receive. I had my first catch in the opening drive. And by catch, I mean drop! Damn! It was my first one of the season. I thought about getting out of the way of the corner who was closing in on me fast, and it took my concentration off the ball. Well, that was that. At least I didn't have the pressure of trying to maintain a perfect catching percentage. That drive we quickly scored. To top it off, I recorded my first touchdown of the season—a 29-yard touchdown pass. My defender played on my outside shoulder. When I passed him, I stuck a skinny post and the ball was right on target. It was a perfect throw. I was happy that Colt and I were on the same page.

It was then our defense's turn. They held the Panthers to a three-and-out. On one of those three, Adam Leonard, our sophomore line-backer, drilled the running back square on his back. It gave me chills! Damn, our defense could hit! It reminded me of when I used to play corner back in high school, the intensity was so high on defense. They let out all their aggression. As receivers, the only thing we can do is try to get a huge pancake block or storm over somebody when we're running. Jason and Ross were masters at doing that; it must be a Samoan thing.

We got the ball back on offense and in no time we scored. This time it was Ross's turn to record his first touchdown of the season—a 16-yard pass to the right corner of the end zone. Back on defense. Immediately we got greedy. Coach Jerry Glanville, our defensive coordinator, called for an all-out blitz. Seconds into the play the Panthers' running back squeaked through the line into an empty secondary. He was home free, or at least he thought he was until 69 yards later he was hawked—caught from behind—by Kenny Patton. How embarrassing to get caught like that! However, the Panthers capitalized on the drive when they scored a touchdown soon afterward.

By the end of the half the score was 34-9. Ilaoa had bulled his way into the end zone, Leonard had a great interception and I recorded my second touchdown of the game. We went into the locker room with a big lead, confident that we were going to win. When I came out of the game I was just so thankful I could do something with the opportunity I'd been given. After the game reporters interviewed me and I got the call-up to the post-game show. I've had plenty interviews before but never after the game in front of a swarm of reporters, cameras and microphones. Usually it was Colt or Davone in that position. I'm sure I sounded like a babbling idiot, with all the adrenaline coursing through my body. But regardless, I went home happy. Six catches for 122 yards and two touchdowns meant next week I was still the starter. I needed to keep up the good work.

▶ OFF THE RECORD

Finding the Silver Lining

Week four was all about opportunity. In football, as in life, opportunities come in several forms. In everyday life an opportunity might arise in the form of a new job opening, an economic boost, a change in location or even a simple "Hi" from a stranger. But opportunity can also come in far less positive ways—in divorces, break-ups and even deaths. In football, more often than not, opportunity comes in the form of injuries. Games aren't postponed or canceled because the star quarterback is sick or injured. Plays will not be re-snapped because a linebacker pulled his hamstring. Life goes on and so does football. So when someone gets hurt, it means that someone else is given an opportunity to play, to start, to shine.

As football players, most of us don't wish for our teammates to get hurt, but at the same time we are completely ready for it to happen. This eagerness is what makes athletes athletes—the want, will and drive to be the go-to-guy.

When a player is thrust into the starting position he has a lot more responsibility and the added pressure of the former starter watching him. How does the sidelined starter cope? Ultimately, it's a question of character, of accepting certain truths in life. The first truth is that bad things like injuries happen to the greatest people, so don't take it personally. Don't sit around the house feeling sorry for yourself. Self-pity is not a reasonable escape. You could blame God, life, Allah or Mother Nature, but in the end, you're only making the road to recovery longer and far more painful. We do not live in a world that caters to us or adheres to our wants, dreams or wishes. That is the first truth you must deal with.

The second truth is that life is not only unfair but it's constant. While you sit there, down and out, there are people doing great things around you. There are games being played and balls being caught without you. Don't get mad, angry or envious about it; that's just the way things are. You have to remind yourself that the world does not stop because you have.

While recovering from your setback, you may hear the age-old maxim, "Everything happens for a reason." This banal saying usually eases the mind and brings a spurious optimism to a seemingly indifferent world. But I would modify that to: "Everything can happen for a reason." With that simple and almost unnoticeable edit, you've taken control of your own life. That brings us to our final absolute truth, which is that things can happen for a reason if you make the effort to find the reason. Use the time away to come back with a full head of steam—seemingly never missing a beat. Use the time to relearn the basics; let the hunger build back up in your heart. Take everything life throws at you and use it as fuel for your zeal, passion and drive.

When someone goes down, it's easy for the next person in line to recognize the opportunity. He has to step up and do his best. When Jason Ferguson was injured in the 2005 season opener against University of Southern California, Ryan Grice-Mullins saw his chance to play—to play great. Then, when Ryan went down in the 2006 Boise State game both Ross and I seized the opportunity to start the entire season.

But what really characterized our Warrior team was our ability to recognize less obvious opportunities. Our team was defined by how we handled our personal challenges. Whether it was a season-ending injury, an academic suspension, unexpected babies or jail time, we found a way to overcome the odds. The great thing about being a Warrior was that despite the setbacks, we came together as a team to do one thing—win.

▶ IN THE LOCKER ROOM

"There were times when I watched from the sideline and I imagined the starter getting hurt. I don't know if I wish for it, but if it happens it happens. That's just being competitive. Or maybe if he got hurt just for a game or two so I could show Coach what I'm made of. I think that crosses the mind of every player, whether they will admit it or not."

"I got hurt last year, but it let me focus on school. It sounds dumb but it's hard to switch football mode off when you have to go to class. Football mode is always on for the entire season. Being a full-time student and football player is hard. But getting injured gave me the time to switch football mode off for a week or two and just focus on getting the grades I needed to be eligible to play football the next semester."

"Getting injured sucks. You work so hard for something … all for what, nothing. You curse at life and just get in bad moods all the time. I don't think most cats know what it's like to work so hard for something, every day of your life and to have it taken away. It's like losing a kid or something."

"As soon as I got hurt, I knew it was something major, otherwise I wouldn't have come out of the game. I was just grateful for the extra year. I used the time to hang around with the guys again, making all the relations."

CHAPTER 6

NEVADA WOLF PACK

▶ **ON THE FIELD**

Tame the Damn Wolf Pack

Game Strategy:
Spread the field and hit 'em hard.

The Wolf Pack of the University of Nevada–Reno was in town, and we knew we had our work cut out for us. Their QB, Jeff Rowe, had a decent arm and their top receiver, a Kamehameha Schools graduate, Caleb Spencer, had returned to the Islands for what he hoped would be a Warrior upset.

We received the ball. Ross caught the kick in the end zone and took a knee. Eighty yards to go; let's do this. The first pass play of the day was to me, a short curl pattern. I loved getting the ball first; I never really felt like I was in the game until I caught my first ball. Davone took the second pass. It was good to get him in the game early. The third pass went to Ross for six yards. Then Davone again for a 30-yard gain. Then Jason had a catch, which got the entire receiving corps into the game as soon as possible. Colt did an exceptional job of spreading the ball around. However, we failed to get a first down and so we left it up to Dan Kelly to kick a 35-yard field goal. Although we hated field goals, we liked the feeling that we could pass on them all day. Colt was already six for six, so it was business as usual with our patented run-and-shoot.

The offensive sat down on the bench and waited for another chance to fully finish a drive, with a touchdown. In no time we found the opportunity, as Nevada quickly answered back with their own successful drive, ending in a TD. On our next series, Colt's first pass should have been intercepted, but we got lucky. Ross caught the ball on a short crossing pattern, then ran over Nevada's No. 23. I loved watching Ross run through people! As we were on the 17-yard line looking to score, Coach called for a fade stop to my side. This was by far the best route to run because it was the hardest to defend. I ran as fast as I could up the field and while the corner ran next to me, stride for stride, I turned around at the last second, reached out behind me and plucked the ball from the air. The drive was textbook! Colt threw a perfect ball to my back shoulder. I caught it, and with my last step in bounds, I reached to get the ball over the orange pylon. Touchdown!

After the point by Kelly, our defense went on the field and forced the Pack to punt. What happened next was perfect. I ran a post in the first play of our third drive. I expected the safety or corner to cover me, but while I was hauling ass downfield, Davone slipped under me toward the sideline. Both defenders went to cover him. One of the great things about having talented players on our team was that when they were not too busy making the highlight reel with their moves and touchdowns, they demanded the full attention of the defense. Nevada busted the coverage and I was home free. I looked back to see if Colt and I were on the same page and the second I turned my head he released the ball. It was one of those plays when I was too wide open. I had all the time in the world to think about anything but catching the ball. I forced myself to remain focused and told myself to catch the damn ball. Before I knew it I was in the end zone untouched for a 40-plus-yard touchdown.

On the ensuing series, our defense, as if refusing to give the offense all the glory, punished Nevada's ball carriers time and time again. Leonard Peters and Jacob Patek forced a fumble and Kenny Patton recovered. If we kept the intensity up we would surely win the game.

We never lost control of the lead against that tough Nevada team. With a 41-34 victory we snuck out with our third win and a .500 record. After the game I sat down and prayed. I thanked God for giving me the chance to shine for the second week in a row. No one but Him could have scripted this better, and I knew it.

▶ OFF THE RECORD

My Very First Testimony

"... please God, let me be injured by the third game of the season ..."

Not many people pray for injury. If anything, most people pray to God that they will remain healthy and fit, and football players are no exception. But for me, in 2005, as I began my next-to-last-season, that wasn't the case. I had come into that season as a starter but I knew that I didn't have enough experience on the field to do anything exceptional. I wanted the chance to play in the first two games against University of Southern California and Michigan State, but I knew that if I played out the entire season my skill level and ability—and more important, my confidence—wouldn't be high enough to play anywhere worthy after college. At the time prayer was new to me. I was more agnostic. I didn't have answers to the many mysteries of the world, and most of my thoughts were logical and rational—in which God wasn't a factor.

It took a conversation with a high school teammate, Cassiel, to get me to pray for the first time. On a hot August day we talked on the phone for hours about life and the nature of God. At the time, I viewed faith as an empowering feeling. It could make the weakest person do incredible and seemingly impossible things. I respected the sanctity and the belief in God, but since it didn't make sense to me, I had no personal belief or faith in God. It was like trying to convince an adult that Santa Claus is real, a hard argument to win. For the most part I felt that religion was a crutch. It was an instrument humans used to make their world feel meaningful—a mere psychological security blanket for which people could blame and thank for whatever happened in their lives.

The conversation with Cassiel reminded me of when I first realized that I didn't believe in God—9th grade. One day I came home and thought real hard about life. I analyzed my feelings and came to the conclusion that I just didn't believe. I was torn by this idea. I was a 15-year-old kid who thought the world was purposeless and cruel. I came home nearly every day, crying and cursing at the people who were blessed with the gift of believing. Immediately I struck out against my parents. I hated the fact that they didn't make me believe. I hated them for not taking me to church enough. I hated them for not giving me the security and happiness that everyone around me had. My hate for them slowly turned into a disdain for humanity. I watched people around me use God as a scapegoat. Eventually, my bitterness toward my parents and others turned into a strong, powerful belief. But not a belief in God or faith; rather, a belief in myself. I decided that for the rest of my life I could do anything I wanted to do as long as I had my own free will. This confidence, a borderline cockiness, became my approach and philosophy toward life.

But back on that August day I dropped all my walls and tried desperately to hear out my friend, Cassiel. By the end of the conversation, he said, "Ian, just pray. Don't do it for me or anyone else, but just pray. Please try it."

I told him I would and we got off the phone. That night I prayed, although at certain times I felt like I was talking to myself. I even had the audacity to open my prayer with skepticism, saying out loud, "God, if you're all-knowing then why do I have to tell you anything? You already know what's in my heart so what a waste of time." But I quickly smothered my inner cynic and attempted to start again. This time I prayed for the health of my family and friends and then I prayed for God to show himself in my life. I prayed for the next couple nights and each time I felt more comfortable. I didn't know if God was actually listening or if simply venting was therapeutic in and of itself. I tried my hardest not to analyze the feelings and sensations. I just let them happen.

Now jump ahead to 2005, right before the new season and the University of Southern California game. Most people would be happy to come in as a starter, but I knew my happiness would be short-lived, because after the season was done I knew I'd be done with football. I had kneeled down the night before summer camp and for the last time I prayed to God to give me more time. I knew that I needed to get hurt by the third game if I was going to be eligible to apply for a sixth year. By now I realized that five years, with all my injuries and time off, was just not enough for me to become a decent college football player. With the start of fall camp I stopped praying. I didn't give up on God, but my mind went right into football mode. I was more worried about keeping my starting job and I was focused on the USC defense more than anything else.

As it turned out, that 2005 season began with two tough losses, the first to USC and the second to Michigan State. Our third game was against a halfway-decent Idaho team. By the second quarter against the Vandals, I was on my way to having a career game. Then I caught a ball, got tackled and landed awkwardly on my knee. I could still play on it so I'd be damned if I was going to come out. I asked the trainers to wrap it up. They told me to remove my shoe. I looked down at my cleats, which were tightly tied with miles of tape, and decided I'd wrap my knee at halftime instead. A couple plays later I caught a pass and headed down the sideline until I was out of bounds. As I took my last step I heard a pop in my knee. It didn't hurt as much as it surprised me. Players often describe injuries as hearing a pop as opposed to feeling it, and it was true. I went to the sideline so the doctor could check me out. I told him it was sore and I'd heard a pop, but it wasn't killing me. I tried to run on it, but I couldn't stop limping. I was out for the game.

On the plane ride home, as the adrenaline wore off and the swelling gathered around my knee I thought about the prayer I'd made to God. I counted on my fingers: 1) USC; 2) Michigan State; 3) Idaho. I couldn't believe it—it was the third game. I tried to rationalize what happened. I thought of everything, but never in my life had a coincidence this big occurred. I was in shock. God had answered my prayer. He was giving me more time. He showed himself to me in the only way He knew I'd listen—a torn posterior cruciate ligament.

God Watches Football

Prayer and religion were all around our team. Before every game, we had chapel. This was a non-mandatory, 30-minute session where the team and coaches heard the word of God. There were also several players on the team who preached the word of God (whether you asked them to or not). Some were a little too fanatical. These guys were usually the ones who had just found or re-found God. In an effort to change their sinful ways they tried their best to be saints. They were quick to let everyone know that they were "saved" and no longer indulged in the shallow spoils of us sinners. Meanwhile, they told us about everything we did wrong. Frankly, it was just annoying. They forgot that pride is a sin, too.

Not all of our religious zealots were preachy. I enjoyed discussions with the more genuine players who grasped what I think God is teaching. For example, Adam Leonard, who educated without indoctrinating. He walked around with his Bible, (with a pigskin, dimpled, football cover) and rationally discussed religion. He didn't pretend to be a saint or without sin. To me, he epitomized one of my favorite verses, "Let him who is without sin cast the first stone." Adam didn't pretend to be an angel. He admitted to his faults and flaws. With a sincere and honest heart, he dutifully tried to find his place in the world. I saw him all the time with the Good Book in hand and with an entourage of open-minded players discussing lessons and teachings from the Bible. He was a man who led not only by example on the field but off the field as well.

"When people come to me to ask about or question God or religion I just give them their options," Adam says. "If they want to accept it, if they want to take that step forward, I'm willing to help them with it."

One night I walked outside my dorm room to find one of my teammates belligerent, bleeding and unable to stand on his own two feet. I looked to see who was holding him up and it was Adam. He was sweating from head to toe, trying to calm down our disoriented teammate. He stood there, struggling to carry 260 pounds of dead weight—all the while praying for our friend's safety. He talked calmly to him, convincing him to go back to his room and just sit down. He made sure that medics took a look at him. By the end of the night our disoriented teammate cried on Adam's shoulder. As bad as this situation might have been, it was a true blessing to witness the power of teammates at work, especially off the field.

"God has always been a part of my life," Adam told me. "He is someone my eyes are always open to, so I might find it easier to accept Him than others. But at the same time, He has His own time; a minute to Him is a year to us—just as long as people know that in each of their lives they have an opportunity to accept Him. But you can't be forced to accept Him. In everybody's life there comes that point in time where you have to choose for yourself. You can't be forced."

▶ IN THE LOCKER ROOM

"The Bible doesn't work in this day and age. You can't expect people not to have sex until they are married. That just ain't natural. I don't know anyone who does that. The Bible is just like a rule book. You're going to break some of the rules, just don't break the big ones 'cause then you're screwed. Hell, I don't know what I'd do without sex. I'd probably kill someone."

"Religion is all around our team. I know I'm not perfect but I do what I can. I know I'm a good person. The worst, though, are those people who try and condemn you, like they are God or something. I don't like to be preached to except if it's from someone who really knows. I remember Coach Jones even preaching on us. He'd say things about the power of Christ and whatnot. But that's one thing I never liked. The underlying theme of all faiths should be acceptance. The end! Wait, Ian, are you going to put my name down?"

"I hate when people pray before games that we come out victorious. The other team is doing exactly the same thing. God doesn't pick sides!"

CHAPTER 7

FRESNO STATE BULLDOGS

▶ ON THE FIELD

What Pleasant Fanfare

"Booooo! You guys suck!" Welcome to Fresno, California, where you'll find the loudest, rowdiest band of blackguards and miscreants in the WAC—the Fresno State University fans. They were the absolute worst, or depending on how you look at it, the best. They knew how to berate, taunt and trash-talk the shit out of us. They were the worst because they had no sense of sportsmanship or dignity, in winning or losing. But on the bright side, these fans were the best because when they tried to trash-talk us, it was just so damn funny. We were surprised by their creativity. It wasn't just Fresno fans either, albeit they were the loudest and most vulgar. Other teams' fans could be just as unique with their material. When we played at Idaho in 2005, a bunch of 12-year-olds who were seated behind our sideline mercilessly teased our long-haired players, pointing out that "the girls' bathroom is that way!" And some fans did their research before game day. In 2004, the Rice University student section was directly behind us, and had gotten wind of quarterback Timmy Chang's baby situation. (Timmy's girlfriend was pregnant.) They kept yelling, "Hey Timmy, how's the baby?" or "Timmy, way to get her knocked up!"

But in Fresno, we got trash-talked from the second we left the locker room to take the long walk down to the field. As we opened the door, the Fresno State marching band hit us with several short musical numbers, each ending with a punctuated, "You suck!" After passing the band, we braced ourselves for the more personalized attacks from fans who didn't like our hair, weight, number, momma, daddy and anything else they could think of. However, walking the line was a great way to get ready for the game. We loved trash-talkers. Keep the hate coming, because any good player will just use it to fuel the fire. There is nothing better than shutting up teams, coaches and the fans, too. And the ultimate conquest is to shut up the entire university town on its homecoming game day.

It was insulting to be the team scheduled for a school's homecoming. It was Fresno's way of telling us that we were going to be a breeze, that they could beat us like they did in 2004, 70-14. We were a team to be taken lightly. They could get the victory and continue their celebration way into the evening. Little did they know that we had brought our own party hats and dancing shoes and just loved a good ol' Bulldog homecoming bash.

Game Strategy:
Don't make Fresno another Boise.

We won the toss. We jogged out onto the field to get ready for another day at the office. Our plan was to score first and never stop. But Fresno had a different idea. Instead of reaching the end zone we couldn't even get 10 yards. Fresno, with all their trash-talking and hollering, made us go three-and-out on our first possession.

It was now Fresno's turn to try to put up numbers. On a deep pass over the middle their giant tight end effortlessly bounced off our defenders and ran the ball 75 yards into the end zone. Our defense looked like a joke out there. Their crowd went wild and it looked as if we were playing the same game we had two years earlier.

We went back on offense and we knew we had to kill their momentum. We calmed down, relaxed our minds and just played ball. We forgot about revenge and trash-talking and blocked out the hype. At the end of that drive Nate was sent into the end zone for our first score of the game. Our offense was getting into it. We just prayed that our defense was, too.

Our defense took the field. First down—we stopped them. Second down—we stopped them. Third down—a long ball missed its target and our defense held them to a three-and-out. Perfect. We got the ball back and on the first play Colt scrambled for the first down. A couple of plays later with another third down we called a switch play. Ross and I were lined up tight to the right side and I was stacked right behind him. The defense shifted and immediately Ross yelled out, "Check alert! Check alert!" I quickly scanned the defense and Ross was right, it was four-across man, which meant they were planning an all-out blitz! At the snap of the ball I adjusted my pattern from a deep post to a quick slant. As with any good team, our QB and linemen read the blitz. The line picked up the blitzing backers and Colt quickly released the ball to hit me right in stride. I slid off a would-be tackler and had a 40-yard sprint to the end zone. It was a perfect example of how we were becoming a fine-tuned team. No assignments were blown and everyone executed perfectly, including Davone who was on the other side running his defender to the end zone. We were up 14-7.

The Bulldogs got the ball back but they didn't keep it for long. Solomon Elimimian forced a fumble, which gave our offense the chance to put together another drive capped by a Nate Ilaoa touchdown. Fresno got the ball back and fumbled again. Our defense was all over it! As we jogged to the huddle for the start of another series I looked around and everyone was smiling. It was then and there when we all knew our team could be great. We felt unstoppable.

At that very point the season became fun. Basketball players often describe the feeling of releasing the ball and knowing it's "nothing but net." They talk about being in the zone and how much fun it is. That day it wasn't just me or Ross or Nate who was in the zone but the entire team. It's much more impressive when an entire team is in the zone. Colt was throwing blocks, receivers were smashing defenders, and our defense was looking to kill. Even Coach Jones joined in on the fun. We rarely call trick plays; we hardly ever do anything out of the ordinary. But at one point, when we were yards away from the end zone, Coach called a fake option. Fresno's defense was keying on Nate so we faked the option to the right side. I went out to my corner, pretended to block for a second, then released into the end zone. Colt faked the pitch to Nate and lobbed it to me in the end zone. Touchdown! On that day, there was only one zone and we were all in it.

I went in a little before halftime to get an IV. I was cramping up so I wanted to fully hydrate. As I walked in the trainers told me that Leonard Peters just made an interception for another touchdown. It was the best we played all season! I went into the locker room and saw that Kenny Patton, our starting cornerback, was already in with his shoulder pads off. I asked him what happened—why wasn't he out there? He told me that it looked like he had broken his collarbone, an injury I was all too familiar with. I sympathized with him; with all the good things happening, it was hard to see something like that. He wasn't totally down and out about it though. Maybe it hadn't set in yet—the realization that his injury was a season ender. Or maybe it was that Kenny knew injuries were part of the game and there was more to life than just football.

More to life than football? Like what? As we all boarded the plane, boasting a 68-37 victory over the 'Dogs, there was nothing in our lives but football. That was all we could think, talk and dream about. But as our natural high started to wear off somewhere over the Pacific, another thought was creeping in. It had nothing, and yet everything, to do with football—it was school. Shit! It was already our sixth game; we were nearly halfway done with the semester, which meant it was time to face one of our toughest opponents—midterms. Most of us didn't even know the location of our classes, let alone the midterm material.

▶ **OFF THE RECORD**

Class? What's that?

We were back in the 808 and it was time do a lot of catching up. When we first signed up for classes most of us tried to get lenient professors and elementary courses. And to be honest, football players have every advantage. We have advisors, mentors, tutors and others. Our team advisors, like Sarah Nunes-Atabaki and Stephanie Miller, sometimes seemed to care more about our education and future then we did. They worked day in and day out to make sure we attended the right classes and that we were on schedule to graduate. Essentially, they were a huge reason why we passed, and they were the only reason that many of us stayed eligible. There were only three advisors working with hundreds of student-athletes, and they didn't even get free tickets to our games. I guess the athletic department felt that they were satisfied to just do a good job.

To help the advisors there were tutors and mentors. The mentors, with whom we could meet weekly or bi-weekly, helped manage our time. They had copies of our syllabi so they knew our assignments, reading material and exam dates. Mentors made sure we didn't get too far behind in our work. But when we did fall behind—sometimes far, far behind—they made sure we did everything that was necessary to catch up. Tutors, on the other hand, helped us directly with all of our subjects. There were tutors for Spanish, Japanese, Economics, Sociology and English. There were tutors to help write papers, solve equations and assist with computer programming. Regardless of our class or major, there was a tutor who had already taken the course or knew everything about the topic.

These tutors weren't all bookworms either. Our most distinguished tutor, who helped with an array of subjects, was Red, who sported more tattoos than any of our Polynesian team members. He always found an answer to our questions, from Psychology to Physics. (He was also the go-to guy when you were trying to solve the school's daily crossword puzzle. He was one of the few who would know the answer to five down—an eight-letter word for "ecdysiast" beginning with S and ending with R.)

With all of this support, it was very difficult to fail school, as long as we went to class—but hey, there's the rub. For me, going to class was by far the hardest part of college. Once I was in the classroom, most of the information slowly seeped into my head, either by way of osmosis or repetition. But the act of going to class was a challenge. Just imagine waking up at about 5:30 a.m. to go to a long two-hour practice, then sitting through hours and hours of boring/pointless/not useful (take your pick) lectures. It's not the practice that kills you, though. It's the breakfast right after practice. When you work out hard for two hours, then shower, you feel refreshed and ready to start your day. But then you sit down and eat some eggs and pancakes and drink a nice, cool fruit punch. Sitting there, your eyes start to feel heavy. The local guys call it a Kanak Attack. You want nothing more than to sleep. So you tell yourself, "My class doesn't start till 10:30 a.m. I have time to lie down for a 10-minute nap." You walk into the training room, or maybe your dorm, to lie down. You close your eyes and it's over—you can forget about making it to class. Once your body is relaxed you start to rationalize why you shouldn't go. You tell yourself, "My body getting sleep is more important than learning a little history, right?" You say, "I have that class in two days anyway. I'll just find out what I missed from Ikaika. I think I've seen him in that class." Or better yet, "This will give me a great chance to talk to that pretty Asian girl who sits right next to me. I'll just ask her what I missed. How was her day? What's her number? Perfect!" After a convincing argument you decide it's time to sleep. The only thing that could possibly scare you into going to class is a class check. Every once in a while, any one of the coaches might pay a visit to our classes— typically ones with a lot of football players enrolled—to make sure their players were there. If Coach doesn't spot you in class, be prepared for some big-time running—dawn patrol! That means running at 5:30 a.m., with all the stair climbing you can imagine.

For football players, falling asleep in class can be an occupational hazard during the season. The problem was that we soon realized we had a lot of catching up to do. But that's college for you: last-minute papers, nail-biting exams and grade-A excuses—explaining to our teachers why we were late or absent. Missing class helped us work on our negotiating skills. By the time we graduated we were so good with our words and bargaining powers I bet we could have sold KCCN Birthday Bash tickets to an agoraphobic.

My 5 Reasons for a College Education

Although I missed far more classes than I attended, I have still found countless reasons why going to college was the right choice. Several times during my tenure as an UH athlete I've had the privilege of visiting local high school classrooms to explain to students what athletics was like, but more importantly, what to expect in college. During my visits I explained my five main reasons why college is a perfect choice.

1) It's not painful. The simplest reason to get an education is that it won't hurt. Knowing things about the world and its people and places can only help you grow in life. Also, being away from home helps you become more independent from your parents. What most people don't realize is that an education isn't

necessarily supposed to put information in our heads, but it's supposed to teach us how to make choices. College isn't about programming students. It's about giving young adults information to discern. College should challenge us. If we have an issue we should take a stance, choose a side.

2) To see the world. You don't need to travel the world or study abroad to see the world. Just go to college. At the University of Hawaiʻi I stepped into a different world. Going to college, and especially dorming, gives you the opportunity to make new friends away from home. It's also a chance to meet people unlike yourself. You're introduced to students who come from miles away, from different walks of life. College isn't about walking a mile in another person's shoes; it's about walking at least a couple steps in hundreds of people's slippers.

3) Opportunity. In this case, opportunity comes in the form of not what you know but who you know. While it sure doesn't hurt to be smart when you graduate from college, if you come out knowing the right people, there is no telling how far your connections will take you—an internship at a top law firm, a managerial position at your local retail store or maybe even to another country. In college you'll meet ambitious, driven people and with that kind of positive energy around you, you'll be even more motivated to move ahead in life.

4) Money. Even if you don't enjoy the work, your classes or even your major, the fact of the matter is, college graduates earn more money. Googling information from the U.S. Census Bureau I learned that in the United States if you have a bachelor's degree, you will earn an average of $51,206 a year, compared to those with a high school diploma who will struggle to make $27,915. If you exceed a bachelor's degree, the average annual salary is $74,602, while those without a high school diploma average $18,734. (If you make it to the NFL minimum wage is around $300,000.) Needless to say, the numbers don't lie!

5) The fifth and final reason to go to college is because it's fun as hell. You'll meet hundreds of other young adults; some are serious about their studies and their future careers, but most of them are into having fun, too. Parties, keggers, gatherings, get-togethers, soirees, sororities, fraternities, athletics, associations, clubs—any excuse for ambitious, eager, hormone-driven youngsters to get together you'll find in college. Whether you like square dancing or hip-hop, college is a perfect place to find others that match your interests. Whatever your criteria, college can be your answer. (Of course, I kept this reason PG when talking to the younger school kids.)

XXXXXXXXXXXXXXXXXXXX

CHAPTER 8

NEW MEXICO STATE AGGIES

▶ ON THE FIELD

The Big M-O

How does the saying go—when you're on a roll, you're on a roll? So what happens when it stops? Let's say a tennis ball is rolling down a hill. If you pick it up halfway down, you stop the roll. If you let it go again, the ball will continue rolling but not with the same speed or force, and the end result is not the same. In football we call this "roll momentum," a.k.a. the Big M-O. For a receiver, momentum starts after a big catch; a running back after a nice run; a linebacker after a great tackle. Each athlete is well aware of momentum, so after a catch, run or tackle, we do everything in our power to keep it going. As momentum builds, it partners up with confidence until we feel unstoppable—we are in the zone. The feeling of being in the zone is highly addictive. If you feel it once, you want to relive it again and again. While momentum builds, confidence is not its only companion. So is selfishness. We don't want anything to kill our buzz and ruin our high, including our backup, a teammate, even a friend.

Game Strategy:
Show 'em who the No. 1 passer really is.

The first quarter was over and we were losing. Well, the score was 14-14 but it still felt like losing. We'd only had two successful drives and our defense had given up too many points. We weren't playing like a team. It's hard to explain why things were going wrong, but they were. We desperately needed to get momentum back on our side.

The second quarter wasn't any better. On offense, after a disappointing third down, we jogged to the sideline and watched our defense try to stop Chase Holbrook, the leading passer in the nation. We wanted to show people that it was Colt, and not Chase, who was the top passer in the WAC. I sat on the bench and took deep breaths; the air was different in New Mexico and it was hard to catch my breath. I sat down next to Chad, but I avoided eye contact. I knew he was going to gripe about playing time. Ever since the Alabama game Coach Jones had been rotating wide receivers. That meant that Ross, Jason, Chad and I took turns going in the game. But because of Ryan's early season injury and the position swap for Ross, I was the sole Z receiver while Chad and Jason were still in rotation. Chad's problem was that Jason wasn't always willing to rotate out. As a result, heavy words had been exchanged during the first half, and Chad was left high and dry, and a little lonely sitting on the bench.

As much as I sympathized with him, it was not the time to think about fairness or foul play. It was time to get back into the game. We needed to band together as one team and restore the offense's energy. I turned to Chad and told him to go in for me. I told him I was having trouble breathing. I figured it was a win-win-win-win situation. It gave Jason the playing time he wanted, Chad the reps he wanted, the team the added energy that it needed and it gave me a break that wouldn't hurt.

Some players would have called Jason obstinate. But that same hardheadedness—borderline selfishness—is what made him such a valuable part of our receiving corps. He thrived on building momentum, getting on a roll made him nearly unstoppable.

Whether my decision to sit out a series or two was beneficial I'll never really know, but since we posted a 49-30 victory over the Aggies, I took an ounce of credit.

▶ OFF THE RECORD

The Underground World of Competitive Gaming

So what did most of us players do with our down time? Did we just sit around and sleep? Yeah, a good number of us did do a lot of that.

But for the more adventurous, there were usually two popular activities going on—video games and poker.

Contrary to popular belief, video games are not all fun and games. Inside the Hawaiʻi football team is an underground syndicate designed specifically to crush the spirit and joy out of gaming, and, consequently, any would-be gamer. Anyone who dared to pick up the sticks (game controller) and challenge this select group was quickly humiliated. After losing on-screen, the player suffered through torrents of verbal and emotional abuse and public embarrassment. There were stories ranging from players forced to wear costumes and dresses to school, to others leaving the scene of the game with broken bones and chipped teeth.

With thousands of games to choose from, which ones were most often kept loaded in the consoles of these video elitists? The hottest game on the market was EA Sports' Madden NFL series, ranging from the 2004 season up through 2007. But the gamers also racked up thousands of deaths in Halo and Halo 2. Who was the ringleader of this band of players? No one was too sure. They all acted as individual splinter cells and when they were not beating lesser opponents they jostled for dominance among themselves. Each proclaimed to be the best.

Posing as an avid video gamer, I entered this underground world. I found out that they played wherever they could find a screen and an outlet. The games could happen anywhere at any time. I even witnessed games being played in the airport lobby, where running back Michael Brewster, a master technician and elite player, rewired a film projector to play games on the wall behind the check-in counters. Those guys were addicts, I tell you. While incognito, I stayed undetected in their hostile domain. However, it was only a matter of time till my inexperience showed and I started to feel the heat. With my cover on the verge of being blown, I quickly struck up a conversation with one of the best Madden players this side of the Pacific, Nate Ilaoa. I wondered if he would disclose any information about this exclusive society. Was he really the best?

"I never look at those rankings," he replied. "Whoever is No. 1 is usually what the people say. So if you've heard that I'm up there, then that's all people need to know." I could tell it was going to be like pulling teeth. I needed to know more.

I had heard a rumor that a game of Madden turned into a fist-fight between two football players, ending with a broken jaw. I needed to separate fact from fiction. "It's true," Nate said. "That incident was over Mario Kart on Game Cube. You can only imagine what a game like Madden would do to someone if Mario Kart made a guy throw a fist. Madden is way more competitive."

I asked Nate one last question. "If you are what people call 'one of the best,' what is the hierarchy? Who is sitting at the round table of the Madden elite?"

He took a minute to think, then said, "If there was a place for all the greats, Michael Brewster would be sitting there; probably Marquez Jackson would be sitting at the table as well. But there are others like Jason Rivers who would be serving us food. Jazen Anderson would probably be vacuuming the rug. That's the picture I see at the Madden banquet."

I knew enough. I had the names of the greats and knew who to stay away from if I ever wanted to play a nice, friendly game of Madden or Halo. But I wasn't sure if I could believe Nate. What if all he told me was a lie? What about the rumors that Jason Ferguson and Chad Mock were among the best? The video game world was a high-stakes, competitive place that had no room for pretenders like me. I was glad to get out when I could. From there I moved into another high-stakes world that I felt a lot more at home in—the world of Texas Hold 'em.

Shut up and Deal!

I left the world of video gaming and took my seat at the poker table. Sitting alongside me were the usual suspects: Hercules "I'll See and Raise" Satele, Samson "We'll See if I Pay" Satele, Dane "The Iceman" Uperesa, Dan "Higher Kicker" Kelly, Kenny "The General" Patton, A.J. "All-in" Martinez and Ryan "Pretty Boy" Keomaka. Throughout the year there were others but none as consistent as these chip-counting champs.

I was first introduced to the poker world in 2004. We were on an away game against Rice University in Texas. I was a rookie at poker but I knew the basics and I was a quick learner. We didn't have any chips to stack so we were forced to use multicolored sugar packets. I played with some of UH's finest—Gerald Welch, Timmy Chang and Chad Owens. I don't remember who won, but after that game I played poker every chance I got.

In August, as soon as summer camp started, poker started. When practice was over we pushed together tables and chairs and played game after game after game. However, further into the season the games got more sporadic and far more exciting. We played in the hotels, airports and airplanes. The main thing for us football players was that there be a defined winner and loser, no matter the game we played. We went as far as tossing footballs into buckets when we ran out of things to do.

"We compete in the dumbest things sometimes," Kenny Patton said. "But being competitive is in our blood; I know I'm going to be doing something competitive for the rest of my life. That's just one reason I play poker."

So who was the big winner during our poker games? Who took home the bragging rights? Me, of course. Well, to be honest, I lost more times than I won. I think the same could be said about most of the regulars. With games sometimes lasting hours, the victor could be a lucky rookie or a skilled vet; it was impossible to predict. But I will give you some insider tips: Don't joke with Kenny when he's losing; he gets pissed. Ryan will play anything and everything; it's rather annoying. Dan will catch whatever he needs on the river so bluff him out of it if you can. When A.J. gets tired he gets reckless and will be all-in with suited connectors. Lastly, Hercules will call if you go all-in with your ace-king. Even if he has a 4-9 off-suit, he'll still beat you with it on the damn river! Talk about annoying! At the end of the day, whether you know everyone's tells, win or lose, the game was always fun.

CHAPTER 9

IDAHO VANDALS

▶ **ON THE FIELD**

The 60s Were a Trip

Week eight was the start of a period I like to call the 60s, which encompassed weeks eight, nine and ten. They're called the 60s because we scored at least 60 points in each one of these games. For three weeks we made post-game party plans as early as halftime. Where was the party, and who was coming? It only made us play better. We knew we had to keep up the scoring if we wanted to follow through with the plans. We didn't want any regrets, on or off the field.

Game Strategy:
Never stop putting up points.

Homecoming night. Even though Hawai'i and Idaho were both 3-1 in the WAC, hosting the Vandals at homecoming told them that we didn't think they were that good. Still, we didn't take Idaho lightly.

As our kick return team jogged out onto the field I asked one of our trainers, Nikki Awaya, to stretch me out. I lay on my back and she stretched my hamstrings. The crowd noise told me that the game was underway. We were receiving, and I guessed that Ross Dickerson would return the kickoff to about the 30-yard line. I quickly jumped up and jogged over to the sideline, ready to go in on offense. As I made my way over, the crowd got louder and louder. I couldn't see past my teammates so I looked up toward the big scoreboard screen and saw Ross streaking down the sideline untouched! We all jumped and yelled. Touchdown! Ross had a 100-yard kick return! The whole team ran onto the field. It was impossible to contain ourselves with that kind of play. It was the best way to start any game.

After the cheers and screams died down, I sat on the bench and snarled at Ross, "Damn it, I was ready to play." Still out of breath, Ross just smiled. He had gotten the momentum rolling for us on homecoming night.

However, in the fourth quarter my own momentum was nearly killed when I was blindsided by a Mack truck. Tyler Graunke had replaced Colt as quarterback. I was running a crossing pattern and Tyler's pass fell short, bouncing on the turf behind me. The next thing I knew I was walloped to the ground. Weren't there rules against running over innocent bystanders? But no flag. I was less concerned about the penalty and more worried about breathing. The wind had been knocked out of me. Finally, I took a huge, painful gasp of air and got back up onto my feet. As I started toward the sideline, I thought: Whoever hit me will definitely have won a victory if I leave this field. I had called for Chad's help, but as he started toward me I began to catch my breath. He asked if I was all right and I gestured to him that I was fine. I lined up for the next play and the ball came my way. I think Coach Jones did it on purpose. I'm not sure, but I was glad that I had the chance to show I was okay. I caught the ball and took another couple good shots from the defenders. But, I got up uninjured.

Getting hit doesn't really hurt. There is too much adrenaline coursing through your body for you to feel any pain. But I do remember smiling when I got up. No one was going to ruin my high. I walked back to the huddle and Samson scolded me, "Stop getting hit, old man!"

By the time the final whistle blew our defense had held the Vandals to a mere 10 points and our offense had amassed 68. Besides, whatever aches and pains I felt were nothing that a night on the town wouldn't help soothe ...

▶ OFF THE RECORD

The Club Scene

Being football players did wonders for our off-field game. Whether we were winning or losing, we were the No. 1 team in the state, with the largest fan turnout. Whether people hated us or loved us, the most important thing was that we were known. And we had girls all around us, willing and wanting.

Earlier in my UH football career, the hot club in Honolulu was Blue Tropix. During the season, places like Blue Tropix, Magoo's, Eastside Grill and Red Lion were declared off limits by the coaching staff. Later on, the favored club spots were Zanzabar and Brew Moon. The highlight of the night at Zanzabar came at 1:30 a.m. when the DJ announced that the UH football team was in the house. When they announced our names, girls' eyes widened and jaws dropped.

▶ IN THE LOCKER ROOM

"Nowadays everyone thinks they are all-stars at the clubs. Freshmen, and people who haven't even seen the field, throw around the Warrior name. When I go to Brew Moon I see even the walk-ons, who just showed up for the first day of practice, wearing stunna shades and trying to act big. These little guys haven't even earned their stripes and they are enjoying the fame and pleasures that we, the ones that have actually done something, deserve. The hype gets to everyone, from freshman to senior. Last year no one even noticed Colt, but now he can't go anywhere without people swarming him. And not just girls...guys, too. Random strangers hug him and everyone and their momma wants to get a picture with him. He can't leave the house without some kind of fanfare. It used to be like that with Mel Purcell, Ikaika Alama-Francis and even back in the day, Timmy Chang. But now, it's the worst it's ever been with Colt. He's got guys, girls, friends and enemies all throwing themselves at him. When we all go out, I just sit back and stay away."

"A lot of the stereotypes come from places like the club. Like how we're cocky and all that stuff. And yeah, maybe it's a little true but we are just out to have a good time. Fun is fun. A lot of people think all we do is disrespect women and whatnot, but honestly, the girls are out to have a good time, too. We know where to draw the line, and if a player crosses it, we will make sure it doesn't happen again. Yeah, we get group mentality sometimes, but we aren't stupid. We know how bad a night, or a career, can get with just one wrong move."

CHAPTER 10

UTAH STATE AGGIES

▶ ON THE FIELD

What's this White Stuff?

Another road trip. It was our last, but by far, our scariest. We headed toward Nowheresville, Utah, late one night. We landed in Salt Lake City and left the plane to board a couple of charter buses that were waiting to take us to our hotel. On a pitch-black night, we made our way to a windy road that was well off the beaten path. The buses made a sharp turn as we ascended to what would be our home for the next couple of nights. We were in the middle of the woods, surrounded by dark trees and strange noises. As our buses climbed the hill, we saw a dim glow coming from up ahead. Upon reaching the faint light the buses stopped and shut down their engines. We had arrived in front of the Bates Motel! Okay, maybe not the Bates Motel exactly, but there were striking similarities—eerily lit windows, looming shadows and no sign of life for miles around. The buses were our only escape, but they had already turned back. The interior of our lodge wasn't any easier on the nerves. It was garnished with grizzled paintings, antique fixtures, spiral staircases and long, dark hallways. The placed looked like it hadn't been touched since the '50s.

Later that evening, in the relative safety of a small dining room, a bunch of us receivers talked about how the hotel was the perfect place for a murderer to hide, or maybe an escaped convict. If there was some crazed psychopath loose, who would die? If we were in the movies, we said, the kicker and punters would be offed first, as they were minor characters. We had each watched one too many horror flicks, and based on their plotlines, we figured that after the kickers were killed, the black players would surely be next. Only half-black myself, I said goodbye to my darker teammates. We knew that Colt, the clean-cut Caucasian quarterback, would make it out alive so we decided to stick with him!

After talking story and laughing off our nerves, we walked back to our separate bedchambers, passing by pitch-dark recesses and doors left slightly ajar. Talking about a killer was a bad idea. By the end of the night a lot of my teammates weren't even sleeping in their own rooms. They doubled up and slept four, five, even six people to a room. Talk about breaking a stereotype. Football players aren't all macho and fearless. That night in Logan, Utah, our Warrior team was transformed into a jumpy, skittish band of five-year-olds.

After a night of tossing and turning and with the death toll still down at zero, we eagerly greeted the morning and ate some breakfast. Several of the guys explored outside the lodge to see what the great outdoors was all about. The woods were not nearly as frightening now, and we discovered patches of cold, wet, white stuff. The Mainlanders didn't pay much attention to it, but the locals ran over and picked it up by the handfuls. It was snow! Since there really wasn't enough of the stuff to make a snowman or snow angels, there was only one thing left to do with our time and the rare frozen precipitation—snowball fight!

We never missed a chance to pick sides and battle one another. There were two patches of snow about 30 yards apart, so geography defined the teams. It was a sight to remember: Most of the football team, wearing nothing but shorts and shirts, heaved snowballs across the field and pretended to be characters from Braveheart or Gladiator.

"Charge!" we yelled.

"Hold the line!" they yelled back.

"Retreat!"

We would have stayed out there for hours if it hadn't been for meetings and film. Through all the fun, we nearly forgot that we had a game to play.

Game Strategy:
Don't let the cold affect us.

It was 46 degrees. 46 degrees! It might as well have been minus 50. We were shivering cold. Coming from the Islands, we had to make sure we stayed loose and warm so we could keep up our winning record. So, how did it go? Well, you already know that the game was in the part of the season called the 60s ... we posted our second highest score of the season, 63 points. Our defense proved they could hold back the Aggies. Utah State scored a field goal in the first quarter and a touchdown in the third—that was it.

While on our way to the win, Colt set two UH records. He threw for 413 yards and six touchdowns. Those six touchdown passes gave him 39 for the year, the most in a single season for UH. He also set the record for the most pass attempts without an interception, 182. Colt was having a season to remember.

After we took a commanding lead in the third quarter, Colt and a lot of the starters were taken out of the game. No point in having them play and risk injury when we already had the game in the bag. In the beginning of the game, the Utah fans seated behind our bench were loud and threatening. But as we slowly buried any hope of their team winning, they became far more docile. Colt spent most of the fourth quarter talking story to one young fan—typical football talk.

However, the highlight of the game, which didn't take place on the field, came when a fan continued to heckle Davone. Since the start of the game, this guy had been making fun of Davone's and Ryan's hair, saying, "Hey, No. 7! You and No. 1 look like Milli Vanilli!"

We sat there on the sideline and tried not to laugh. The same fan called out to our smallest receiver, Mike Washington, "Hey, No. 5, you look like Webster!"

We couldn't hold it in any longer; we cracked up. That fan was on a roll. By the fourth quarter the fan curbed his witty quips and engaged Davone in a normal conversation, asking, "Where you from? What year are you?" Stuff like that. Then the fan asked, "Hey, No. 7, what are you majoring in?"

Knowing the fan probably still had some jokes up his sleeve and not forgetting the entire three quarters of harassment, Davone said, "Y.B."

"Y.B., what's that?" the fan asked.

"Ya bitch!" Davone exclaimed.

The entire section within earshot, including our sideline, burst out laughing. It was the first time I saw one of our players embarrass a fan. It was hysterical.

After beating Utah State (and their fans), we clinched a bid to the Sheraton Hawai'i Bowl, to be played back at Aloha Stadium on Christmas Day. It was a great feeling knowing we had a post-season. Not to mention my dad had come out to Utah from New Jersey for the game, a total surprise. I especially wanted to rise to the occasion. So how did I do? I dropped two passes (one of them for a sure touchdown) and sat out for most of the game. I blamed it on the drugs …

▶ OFF THE RECORD

The Trouble with Needles

I started getting familiar with the needle during the Nevada game. It was something I had to do and the doctors said it was okay. Other players did it, too. I'd walk into the room and they would close the door and put the needle in my veins. It felt cold as it entered my body and by the time it was all over, I felt revived and ready to take on the world. I'm just talking about an IV with saline solution, of course.

I got so dehydrated during games and lost so much water that I made it a habit to get an IV at halftime or before the game. Since high school I'd had trouble staying hydrated. I cramped up nearly every game. I drank what seemed to be gallons of water till my stomach was on the verge of exploding but it didn't stop the cramps. The doctors said I needed more salt in my diet, but that didn't work either so I became accustomed to getting IVs.

Before the Utah State game I felt under the weather. I blamed the snowball fight, when I wore just shorts, slippers and a T-shirt. Not one of the smartest moves, considering I had lived in cold weather for years and knew how sick I could get by being underdressed. Regardless, I thought that getting an IV would help restore some of my energy and spunk. Except I didn't count on losing blood when they hooked me up. For whatever reason my veins didn't feel like cooperating and I came out of the IV feeling dizzy instead of refreshed. I thought I could shake it off. It was a momentary sensation but anyone watching could tell I wasn't myself. I had trouble getting off the jam from the cornerback, who was half my size. I dropped balls because I couldn't focus. Pride got the best of me, and I stayed in longer than I should have. I thought, "Shit, my dad is here. I have to do better." But my body didn't let me.

At least we won. That was the last time I got an IV. It was nothing against its effectiveness, but I didn't want to have a repeat of that Utah State game, so I just stayed away from the needle. I decided that good ol' fashioned drinking was the best way to stay healthy.

CHAPTER 11

LOUISIANA TECH BULLDOGS

▶ **ON THE FIELD**

Caging Another Dog

Game Strategy:
Win without Nate.

Louisiana Tech had beaten us 46-14 the previous year, so it was time to show the 'Dogs the new us. We were ready to run up the score. At the time, we led the nation in scoring offense, passing offense, total offense and passing efficiency, while Tech was 119th (dead last) in total defense. Not good for them.

They received the opening kickoff. Their offense came out onto the field looking to score. The Bulldogs' offense was similar to ours so our defense was used to seeing schemes like theirs in practice. But our defense played soft. Tech reached the red zone and kicked a field goal that put them on the board first, 3-0.

On offense, our first drive lasted longer than we were used to. It took 10 long plays to score a touchdown. I noticed myself breathing harder than usual. Then it clicked—Nate hadn't been in! The great thing about Nate Ilaoa was that you knew that when it was a running play, he was not only going to do something amazing, but he was going to gain a lot of yards. No wonder we were working harder than usual; Nate wasn't in. After Regan Mauia barreled into the end zone, I ran off the field and yelled at Nate. "Why the hell aren't you playing? I'm out of breath out there."

He laughed because he knew I wasn't really pissed. He said that Coach had benched him due to an injury he got during the week. He probably could play but only if we really needed him.

Tech got the ball back and our defense stepped up their game, holding them to a three-and-out. With a semi-successful drive on offense we mustered out a field goal. Despite not reaching the end zone, we started to pull away. We watched from the sideline as our defense took the life force out of the Bulldogs. Leonard Peters laid the hat on their running back No. 38. Damn, it sent shivers down my spine. Since it looked as if our defense was going to stop them, I went to the bench to pick up my helmet. Just then their tight end scored! Right down the inside seam. Our defense was great, but somehow we always had trouble with those big-ass tight ends!

With the second quarter winding down and with one minute and eight seconds left on the clock, we went into a no-huddle offense. We had 80 yards to go. First play, quick out to Rivers—completion. Deep slant to Rivers—completion. Dropped ball by Ryan. Leaping sideline catch by Davone in triple coverage—completion. Missed touchdown catch by Davone—they had good coverage on him. At second-and-20, Rivers ran a streak down the sideline, Colt found him open—touchdown! We all cheered until we saw a flag on the field. Apparently Rivers had been pushed out of bounds and the referees said he stayed out too long before coming back onto the field of play. It was bullshit. If anything, the referees were using this as a make-up call. They must have thrown an unjust flag against Tech earlier. This happened all the time. On third-and-20, Regan then caught the ball on a short shuffle pass and made a highlight run to get the first down. With three seconds left on the clock, Kelly chipped in a field goal from the seven-yard line. We went into to the locker room at halftime with a disappointing three points but we knew the game was ours if we continued to drive the way we had in the last minute.

We talked to Coach Jones about the schemes. We told him how Tech wasn't doing anything we couldn't handle. When Coach left, one of us asked the important question, "Yo, what's good for tonight?"

Knowing we had plans to celebrate after the game we marched back out onto the field and outscored them 35-7. In this second half I witnessed the best catch I'd see all season. Ryan Grice-Mullins, who had returned weeks earlier off of a high ankle sprain, made the highlight reel on a deep streak pattern. He ran down the far sideline. Bulldog No. 21

had perfect coverage on him, but he was playing man so he didn't have his eyes on Colt. Colt, who knew that Ryan could adjust to the ball and that there was no chance of having it picked off, heaved the ball into the air. It was slightly underthrown so Ryan dipped right under the defensive back and made a sliding catch. I was on the other side of the field and said under my breath, "Oh … my … God." I wanted to make an outstanding catch like that. I had a chance later on that same drive when I reached behind me to reel in a three-yard touchdown reception. Maybe it wasn't as good as Ryan's, but I'd take it!

▶ OFF THE RECORD

Watch Out for Pro Ho's and Jersey Chasers

What are pro ho's and jersey chasers? These are the girls that only date and hook up with athletes.

Where are they located? At any major sporting event. They can be found late at night around the dorms, major clubs and select house parties.

What are their intentions? Some just want to be with and around athletes—in this case, Warrior football players. But some go as far as dating, sex and drama.

How do you spot one of them? It isn't easy with the naked eye; you don't want to get them confused with your average, run-of-the-mill female fan. But keep in mind that jersey chasers typically travel in packs.

Do they want your money? Some of them may be gold-diggers, but on the collegiate level these women typically aren't as interested in your money as they are in your fame.

How do you avoid them? Lock yourself in your room and don't show up at practice, games, clubs or any social scene. In other words, you can't.

Well, what do I do when I see one, or worse yet, if one talks to me? Avoid eye contact at all cost, but if it's too late, then engage in normal conversation. The best way to make one of these women lose interest is to talk about school or your girlfriend who you are madly in love with back home. You can even go as far as telling them you're gay (I've done that; it works wonders). The most important thing is to make sure you don't seem interested in them.

Should I bring any protection against these women? Bring your will power and make sure there is no alcohol in your system.

What if I feel myself falling into her trap? Fight it, fight it and fight it some more, but if you feel like you're in a losing battle, then give it up. Let me just say that these girls are experts in all aspects of their game, so sit back and enjoy!

▶ IN THE LOCKER ROOM

"There's this one group, there are five girls, and they're official groupies. They even got stickers on their cars that say it. I've never seen hotter girls anywhere. I even heard that one of them tried to date Timmy Chang back in the day. The girls just try for whichever player is the most popular at the time. They might be groupies, but they got control when they're that good looking."

"Man, you can find groupies anywhere; they don't have to be the club type and those kinds of girls. We live on lower campus with all the other athletes. So athletes are our community; these are the people we usually chill with and whatnot. So even other athletes can be like groupies, even more so because they actually know who we are and what we do. You're not only a name, not just a football player, but they see us almost every day so it's almost like being with us is more acceptable."

XXXXXXXXXXXXXXXXXXXX

CHAPTER 12

SAN JOSE STATE SPARTANS

▶ ON THE FIELD

Spartans vs. Warriors

San Jose State ruined it! They'd had a chance to beat WAC front-runner Boise State the previous week and they let it slip away. We could have been at least co-champions if they had won. Oh, and for that to have happened we would have had to beat the Spartans today. We still had hope, though. If we could beat San Jose and if Nevada could upset Boise next week, we were in. But enough with the calculations. The fact that San Jose had barely lost to Boise showed that they were a formidable team—one to be reckoned with.

This game was a battle of two Oakland players. Davone Bess, arguably our best player, and their best player, running back Yonus Davis, had both played for Skyline High School in Oakland, California. In high school, Davone's quarterbacking skills and Davis' running—1,208 yards and 16 touchdowns—had led Skyline to its league championship. With no such help today, Davis and his San Jose State Spartans still planned to upset what could be our eighth straight victory. After both players exchanged pleasantries in the end zone—both still sporting their trademark Bay Area long dreads—the game was underway.

Game Strategy:
Readjust to playing hard teams.

From the first drive we knew the Spartans weren't anything like the last three teams. Led by Dick Tomey, the popular former UH head coach, San Jose State meant business, especially on the defense. From the get-go, gaining yards was a battle. Chad Mock scored our first touchdown of the game in the first quarter. I always got amped when Chad scored. He didn't see the end zone as often as the other receivers, so it was great when he paid it a visit. When the whistle blew signaling the end of the second quarter, we were only up by 10. Making matters worse, Samson Satele continued to scuffle with one of the Spartans' defensive linemen. Several of us held Samson back, reminding him we had a game to play, but when he got pissed he was hard to control. A couple months earlier, for example, Alonzo Chopp had been shooting his mouth off about a running workout. Samson told him to shut up but Alonzo continued to talk. Bad idea. Samson charged his way through several of us to confront Alonzo. I got between the two and with one arm Samson sent me flying backwards. In one stunning instant I realized Samson's strength. I might as well have been a gnat!

Now with the entire team suited up with pads, we had to make sure Samson didn't do anything rash. Thankfully, he chilled out during the second half and became the driving force as we gained control of the game. Colt threw four straight touchdown passes and our defense held Yonus Davis to a pathetic 29 yards on 14 carries. The only star from Skyline High School that day was Davone Bess, who managed to catch six passes for 81 yards and two touchdowns.

▶ OFF THE RECORD

From Prison to Paradise

This is the point in the book where I tell you a story. It's one of those heart-warming, character-revealing tales. It starts with a young boy growing up in the busy streets of California, where chances are few and failure is always at hand. At a young age he picked up athletics— basketball and baseball were his sports of choice. By his sophomore year in high school he became a year-round athlete and an immediate standout in football. As he entered his senior year his football coach told him that he needed to watch his grades, take the PSATs and stay out of trouble. His coach realized that he had a gifted athlete on his hands, one with the ability to play college football. Up until this point the boy had never put college into the equation. Like many teens, planning ahead was not a priority, but he liked the idea of college and what it could do for him. His coach wasn't the only one who wanted to see him escape his troubled neighborhood. His mother also pressed him to leave, as there were so many other possibilities out there for him.

His hard work paid off. By the end of his senior season he signed a letter of intent with Oregon State. He was heading to a four-year school on a full-ride football scholarship. He was going to enter the privileged world of the student-athlete. By escaping a school troubled with race relations and a city burdened with crime, he would discover a college lifestyle that was dedicated to higher learning and better living. However, he wasn't quite ready to leave his home and friends. During the summer, two months shy of his first collegiate semester, he got a call from some buddies. He knew they were up to no good. He knew they were carrying stolen merchandise. But loyalty was blind, so against his better judgment, he went along anyway. Ten minutes after picking his friends up, the police pulled him over. The cops searched his car and found the stolen goods. His friends could have said it was theirs. They could have said he had nothing to do with it, but it wouldn't have mattered. Possession is nine tenths of the law.

For months he was shuffled back and forth between detention center and court. The judge refused to release him during his hearings so going home wasn't an option. He was facing up to 15 years in prison. His life was shattered. No more school, no more football. The window of opportunity had closed. After a long process, the judge sentenced the young man to 15 months in jail. While most people would have broken down faced with spending more than a year wasting away in jail, he was relieved to have eluded the maximum 15-year sentence. His friends got off easy. Some of them only spent a couple of months in jail, others were released even sooner. To make matters worse, the "celebration" of his 18th birthday fell during the hearings and trials. But there was no time for cake and cookies. The only present waiting for him was from the California legal system, and it wasn't juvenile hall or a detention center, it was jail—he wasn't a kid anymore.

When he first got to jail he was on 24-hour-a-day lockdown. He had to stay in his cell for 23 hours at a time, to be let out an hour a day to walk around. His roommate was a 60-year-old man; his jail cell small and dingy. He asked God, "What am I doing here?" It would have been easy for him to give up. To rot in his cell and listlessly wait for whatever life brought him.

Word on the street back home was that his life was as good as over; his efforts had been all for nothing. As the weeks and months faded away, so did his name and reputation. The only contact he had with the outside world was through his only visitor; his mother. The life he had once lived with such enthusiasm and loyalty had turned its back on him. He was just another urban statistic.

Most people behind bars lose hope. Men are like candles, burning bright and strong when they are in the open air. But cover them with glass, trap them behind bars and slowly their fire is snuffed out. It is only the few, the miraculous, who continue to shine bright. He was about to learn in his cramped cell if he was one of those few.

Since his original plan was shot, he took a journal and started to plot plan B. He knew that many colleges wouldn't accept a kid who'd been to jail, so he would have to think of another way. He did not spend his time feeling sorry for himself, instead he wrote about his options. When he got out he could go to a junior college, work his way back up to a four-year institute, earn a scholarship, get a degree. To come up with new plans, he used the only tool he had—hope. He used it everyday, all day.

While he patiently sat in his cell waiting for a chance to start anew, wheels in the free world were already being put in motion. He wasn't the only one who was not giving up hope. His high school coach, John Beam, knew not only what kind of athlete he was but also what kind of person he was. He was a survivor, and when it was time for him to leave prison, his coach wanted to see him hit the ground running—literally. Beam knew a former football player at Skyline High School who had just finished playing football for Hawai'i and was now a graduate assistant. Beam told the grad assistant, K.B., that the Warriors needed to recruit this athlete, despite his miscues. K.B. flew to California and got the young man a temporary release. For the first time in more than a year, he was able to throw on some cleats and momentarily remember what it was like to play football—to be free. During this "tryout" K.B. filmed him doing drills and catching balls. He was a little rusty, but he gave his all with the brief time he had. It seemed like as fast as K.B. had come, he was gone again and our young man was back in his cell. Everything from that point on was out of his hands.

What exactly went through June Jones' head when he decided he wanted this kid with so much baggage is uncertain. Maybe a winning record was the only thing on his mind. He knew that the kid was a steal—a Pac-10 recruit would do wonders for his up-and-coming program. Or maybe, it was all about second chances. Coach Jones, who nearly lost his life in a car accident in 2001, knew that life rarely gives do-overs. Whatever his reasons, he wanted this kid out of jail as soon as possible. He tried to get him released earlier but the law offered no leniency; he was to stay in jail for the full length of his sentence.

Now our boy, who quickly became a man during his incarceration, waited as the days and weeks slowly ticked away. He waited until September 2004, when he was finally freed. While other colleges wouldn't even think about signing a kid that had just spent more than a year in jail, Hawai'i wanted him—Hawai'i was his second chance.

Davone Bess enrolled at the University of Hawai'i in January 2005. From the moment he stepped off the plane he made waves on the gridiron—reception after reception, run after run. From the instant I saw him catch his first punt in practice I knew he was going to be something good. Coach must have seen the same thing. I'm not quite sure what makes a great athlete. It must be a mixture of speed, strength, poise, awareness, quickness, intelligence, determination, will and coordination. It's not an exact science. There is no formula for what makes someone great. But when I saw Davone catch that first punt, I knew he was.

"Being out here in Hawai'i," he told me, "It's a blessing, dawg. I just don't take anything for granted. I know what it is to be at the very, very bottom. Being down to your last dollar on commissary."

As the months and years passed, I grew to know Davone. In practice, games, meetings and clubs I started to learn who Davone really was. But it wasn't until our 2006 season when I was reminded of Davone's background. In Boise, Idaho, our Holiday Inn had a ping-pong table and Davone and I played a few fun matches. When we returned to Hawai'i, we found a table on campus. It was only a matter of time for us to take our competitiveness to a different sport. It was a tradition for the remainder of the season for the two of us to go down to the Noelani dorm lounge and serve up several games. (And don't let him tell you otherwise—by the end of the season I came out on top!) I admired the way he played ping-pong much like I admired the way he played football. He knew how to put spin on the ball; he had finesse and pizzazz when he played, while I was the more traditional, defensive player, just making sure to return the ball and wait for my opponent to make a mistake. Not many people know how to play ping-pong, at least play it well, but he did. I told him I learned how to play at the community pool when I was a kid. When my friends and I were tired of swimming we'd go play ping-pong. I asked him where he learned. And as he slammed the ball with his paddle, and sent it bouncing off my side of the table and whizzing past my ear—he said, "Jail."

At the time I knew he had been in jail but it had slipped my mind. We laughed it off and I went on to win the game (despite what he may tell you). I thought about how far he had come, from having nothing to deserving everything. He was a freshman All-American on his way to breaking NCAA records. His No. 7 jerseys were in all the stores and thousands adored him! But I don't sit here writing about Davone because of his trials and tribulations. I do it because Davone Bess is my inspiration.

And I choose my words carefully when I say "inspiration." Most people could admire him, which is great. To be admired is fulfilling; people take notice of your qualities of greatness. Some would envy him. I see envy as the point where admiration turns to jealousy, but it's still a compliment. However, inspiration is a word that has no equal. While envy and admiration are flattering, they are also static. Davone's character moves me to become a better football player. He inspires me to handle public acclaim with the same grace that he shows. He inspires me to do everything in my life with such reverence that my character is defined by it.

He inspires me because despite all the accolades he earns, I have never seen a person carry himself with so much class and modesty. Being the No. 1 receiver comes with hundreds of perks. He could have taken plays off or missed practices, but instead he was out on the field every day hours before any of us stepped into the locker room. He caught hundreds of balls on the Jugs passing machine before we even touched the field. His strive for perfection not only set him apart as a football player but as an individual.

One day in November, Davone asked if I could help him with a research paper. That evening I sat down with him and looked over the guidelines for the assignment. After I read it for the fourth time, I finally grasped what his professor was asking. I told Davone how involved it was going to be. (If an English major has trouble just figuring out the guidelines, you can imagine how challenging the whole paper was going to be.) I told him I'd look over the instructions some more and get back to him in the morning.

At the time, I only had two classes so I figured I could tackle this research paper on my own. The next morning I told Davone that I could either do the entire project for a fee or I could tutor him whenever he needed it, for free. To me, it really wasn't about the money. I gave him the choice because I was more interested in what he'd have to say. Without hesitation Davone said, "Nah, I can do it."

He understood that he'd have to handle weeks of work, days of dedicated library time and countless hours of reading, writing and researching, and still he said, "Nah, I can do it." Not to mention, it was the busiest and most important part of the football season, with Big Ten and Pac-10 teams flying in to play us. Davone was the epitome of hard work.

When Davone is in the later years of his life I pray that he'll come to me with that same genuine smile and the same optimistic look in his eyes and ask, "Samps, I'd like you to write my entire story."

And before I do it, I'll invite him over, hand him a paddle and ask, "Shall we continue where we left off?"

▶ IN THE LOCKER ROOM

"If other people were as popular as him, they'd be cocky. There are plenty of people on the team that get good and then stop working hard. Other receivers have had the same popularity and their whole personalities change. They think they're the shit. But Davone is still the same person. He's still a homey."

"Davone's an athlete, man. He's good at basketball, too. He can do things that others can't and he plays at a level that others only dream about."

"I wake up to go to the locker room, Davone's already in there. I come back from class, Davone is still in there. That's part of what makes him so good. If he's not out on the field, he's up watching film or hanging out somewhere else around the athletic complex."

CHAPTER 13

PURDUE BOILERMAKERS

▶ ON THE FIELD

We checked our phones in the locker room, praying that Nevada beat Boise State. It was our last chance to take co-ownership of the 2006 WAC title. Before the game started, though, one of our receivers, Dylan Linker, gave us the heart-sinking news that Nevada had lost. Damn it, second place sucks!

We weren't the only ones with our heads elsewhere. Purdue's head coach, Joe Tiller, didn't want to be playing this game. He didn't want to be in Hawai'i. It was too humid. It was Thanksgiving weekend. It was a waste of time. Truthfully, we all needed to pull our heads out of our asses. This game was going to happen regardless. We all had to just shut up and play.

Game Strategy:
Beat the Big Ten and enter the Top 25.

With the WAC co-championship out of our grasp, we still had an important goal this weekend: to crack the national Top 25. We were right on the verge, and we were confident we would make it if we beat the Big Ten's Purdue University.

But that Saturday night, the Boilermakers were making great catches and clutch plays. Our offense turned the ball over several times. We were too comfortable going in at halftime, up by 17. Their defensive ends were good, maybe too good. They rushed hard and fast, throwing off Colt's drop back, making him scramble here and there. We lost the lead and found ourselves late in the game down 35-27, with the ball deep in our own territory. Reagan came through with a huge third-down run.

We needed the run to work because Colt was under pressure, throwing in a hurry and forcing his passes.

The ball was snapped and Colt threw it over the middle to Davone, who was in triple coverage. Davone plucked the ball from the air. Time was not on our side. Colt then threw a pass to an open Jason Rivers, who made a great catch and run. In six plays we drove 71 yards. From five yards out Ryan faked right then dipped under his defender to the left, leaving him in his tracks. Colt found him wide open in the back of the end zone! Touchdown! We needed to go for two. Colt hit Ryan again, this time on a quick out. It was all tied up at 35-35.

Our defense needed a huge stop. Purdue came out in what looked like a four-receiver set. They were going to pass. Their quarterback, Curtis Painter, was 11 for the last 11! Our crowd was going wild: Defense! Defense! The ball was snapped; from the sidelines we screamed, "Pass!"—followed by a sack by linebacker Blaise Soares. After another stop our defense needed to hold them on a crucial third down. On the sideline we all prayed, "One more stop, D, please, one more stop." Purdue was six-for-six in their last third-down conversions. We were all nervous. Painter called hike, dropped back in the pocket and threw a deep pass to a receiver streaking down the sideline. He overthrew and Gerard Lewis, our starting corner, slid in to make the interception!

Offense quickly jogged out on the field; our defense had given us life! The next two minutes and twenty-seven seconds were going to go down in UH football history. On the first play, Jason Rivers caught a pass and barreled into the Purdue 41-yard line. Next play, Colt threw again to Jason, who beat his man to the end zone! The ball fell off his fingertips; almost had it. It was second and 10. Colt made another completion to Jason for a 14-yard gain. Jason was in the zone, talking shit—this is football!

It was the first down on the 27-yard line. We felt the excitement and adrenaline pumping through our veins. It didn't matter who Colt threw to, momentum was building in every single one of us. Colt rolled out, he was in trouble, he tucked the ball and stepped out of bounds on the 23-yard line. One minute and thirty-four seconds to go. Colt jogged to huddle, "460," he said. That was my play, a screen to the Z-receiver. Colt told Dane Uperesa, our right tackle, to make sure the defensive end's hands stayed down, don't let him deflect the ball. The ball was snapped, and I ran down the line. I couldn't see Colt—the linemen were in the way. Then I saw the passing window. Colt almost threw but the window closed. I shuffled to slide into the next one, Colt released the ball and it hit my hands. I caught the ball and started running. I followed my linemen, who were yards ahead of me blocking. I saw a crease to the end zone; if I ran my fastest I could reach the corner. Jason was out in front, and he just leveled his cornerback! All my blocks were perfect. I was in the end zone untouched! Touchdown! I leaped into the arms of Vili, our Polynesian warrior mascot. Pure pandemonium! I couldn't even hear myself think, the stadium was so loud. I went to the sideline and I couldn't believe that we had scored and it was my touchdown. But all the same it wasn't me. It was Colt, it was Jason, it was Davone. It was Ross, Chad, Ryan. It was Dane, Sam, Herc, Tala and John. It was our defense. It was the 44,000 fans inside Aloha Stadium.

I sat in awe as our defense took the field. With two minutes to play Purdue captured one last first down before Painter threw a game-ending interception to a wide-open Adam Leonard. "The Hawai'i fans," yelled TV play-by-play broadcaster Jim Leahey, "are on the edge of delirium!" We all ran onto the field. The game was over. We had nine wins in a row and were on the map as a Top 25 team!

▶ OFF THE RECORD

The Darker Side of Winning

I went home after the game and just sat on my bed. My teammates all got ready to go out while I couldn't even force myself to move. I wasn't sore, or even tired—I was humbled. So humbled by the outcome of our game that it left me paralyzed in deep thought. I couldn't reflect enough about what happened. To me it wasn't just a victory, not even a game-winning touchdown. It was something more and I couldn't quite figure out what.

I sat there for what seemed like hours and sifted through my feelings. There was happiness and excitement, but at the same time I felt despair and hopelessness. I didn't know why I felt bad; maybe I knew it was all coming to an end. Maybe I knew that this high was only going to last a few more days, until our next game was underway. Then a new season would come around, and all would be lost.

I slowly slipped into a depression. It drove me crazy to not have an answer, or even an understanding of the problem. I had to get away. I called up my fellow receivers so they could temporarily take me away from my dark thoughts. I needed to go be around them so I could laugh, joke and get out of my funk.

I got ready and waited for Chad to pick me up. With the dismal thoughts still running rampant in my mind, I knew what I had to do. The only way I ever got through anything in life was through expression. At that moment I felt the uncontrollable desire to let those closest to me know what they meant to me and how they affected me.

Those people were my teammates. There and then I decided that before our last game I would give my team the speech to end all speeches. Whether this would help me to slip out of my bittersweet depression, I didn't know and I didn't care. I needed to end the season with my Warriors knowing how I felt. How we were all more than just individuals doing our jobs. How, regardless of will or want, we were all connected. I needed to put a storybook ending on the season so I could have peace of mind, and they could know how I felt about them.

XXXXXXXXXXXXXXXXXXXXX

CHAPTER 14

OREGON STATE BEAVERS

▶ **ON THE FIELD**

No. 24 Team in the Nation

We were the 24th-ranked team in the nation on a nine-game winning streak. Our QB was a Heisman Award candidate, with 51 touchdowns he was four away from breaking the NCAA's single season touchdown record. We were No. 1 in the country in passing yards per game—382.4—and total offense at 410.8 yards per game. We felt on top of the world.

Nate wasn't 100 percent in time for the game with Oregon State, so Ross took his place as running back. As part of this position change, Ross had to wear a different jersey—No. 37. It looked weird on him and we made sure to rag on him about it.

Game Strategy:
Stay on the map.

From our first drive that night, the Beavers brought on the pressure. At first, it was too much for us to handle. It was difficult partly because one of the Oregon State coaches, Mike Cavanaugh, had coached our O-line for six years. He knew every one of our pass protection schemes. But no excuses, it was football—just play. We made some completions but not enough. On a fourth and 23 we sent Kelly in to kick what would have been a 50+ yarder, if he had made it. It was our defense's turn.

On the Beavers' first possession we held them to a three-and-out. It gave us time to adjust to their defense. Unfortunately, our second possession didn't fare much better than our first; another set of downs ended in another missed kick. The score was still 0-0.

On their second possession, the Beavers scored. We didn't think much of it. Even though our last two offensive drives had been unsuccessful, we were building rhythm. Our offense adjusted to the pressure and started to perform. Reagan and Nate were switching off at running back and doing what they did best—making things happen. Nate finished our drive with a touchdown run.

What no one knows is that Nate's touchdown had been seconds away from being a penalty on me. I was supposed to line up off the ball and not till the last second did I remember and quickly step back off of the line. If I hadn't moved it would have been too many men on the line of scrimmage, which would have negated the touchdown. Not to mention, I would have been yanked from the game. It's one thing to make a physical mistake and miss a ball or a block, but Coach Jones hated mental errors. I returned to the bench with a racing heart. I was grateful that I didn't get a penalty and that the team was back in the game.

We felt great until their kick returner took it 100 yards for a touchdown. Shit! Our momentum was just squashed. Their team was well coached. They knew from watching film that we always kicked the ball left and attacked that side. So, when their returner caught the ball he took it down the opposite side of the field where we didn't have as many men. Touché Beavers, touché.

We didn't stay down long. In the next series we drove down the field and Colt ran it in, tying the game at 14. By halftime the score was tied at 21. We went into the locker room and knew we could beat this team. We had made careless mistakes and missed too many opportunities, especially against a well-informed team like the Beavers. We came out at halftime and reveled in the fact that we were typically a better second-half team.

The Beavers received the ball but we stopped them on that opening drive. Our defense came up big and forced them to punt. We got the ball back on offense and drove down the field. With 15 yards to reach the end zone it looked as if we were going to score. Instead, Davone stumbled out of his pattern and the ball was thrown wide, right into the arms of Oregon State's diving safety. We challenged the call but the ruling stood—it was a touchback. The very next play, they threw a deep bomb down their sideline for an 80-yard touchdown. In a matter of two plays we went from almost scoring to being down by a touchdown. It was sickening.

With our defense only lasting for one play, we were back on the field with the same intensity. Nate started us off with a 30-yard run. We needed that momentum. I had a quick screen and lost six yards on the play. Shit, that's the cost of trying to make something happen. I prayed that my one play wouldn't prevent us from scoring. On the following play Colt and Samson bungled the snap and we lost more yardage. We needed to stop making little mistakes because they were going to add up in the long run. It was third and 25, so we gave the ball to Nate. He ran through and over people for a 21-yard gain. We wanted to go for it, since we were only four yards away from the first down, but Coach played it safe. He sent Kelly in to kick. It went directly through the uprights. We returned to the bench pissed off. We hated field goals!

In the fourth quarter Oregon State scored again, when one of their safeties snatched another ball from the air and recorded his second interception. Colt's balls were not as perfect as we were used to. He was pressured by Oregon State's defensive ends and hurried out of the pocket. Their defense was throwing off our rhythm.

Luckily our defense held them, and on their punt they bobbled the snap so we had the ball back with great position on their own 46. We drove all the way down and Ryan scored a touchdown, making the score 35-32—advantage Beavers.

Our fans got louder and we were sure this would be Purdue all over again. We stepped up our game on both sides of the ball. Our defense held them to another three-and-out. Our offense was feeling saucy. On the punt return Davone reeled in a booming kick, gave a spin move, juke, juke and was off to the races! He managed to slip by the punter but was slowed down enough to get tackled from behind. It didn't matter— things were all going our way. Colt called for another screen to me. I thought that I could make this another game-winning touchdown—just run hard and follow my blocks. I caught the ball, made a quick move up the field and saw daylight. Then suddenly I was hit from the side and brought down to the ground. I didn't even see the guy coming; he came up from my blind spot. I quickly got up and was happy that at least we had the first down. Then I felt my hamstring contract. I hated cramping up. It was a long game, I knew that I should have drunk more water. I limped to the bench and cursed my hamstring and the fact that I hadn't seen my tackler. I got up to watch our offense and my other hamstring cramped, I hobbled over to the sideline in hopes of watching us score. But Colt's final passes fell short of his targets. I felt like throwing up. Oregon State was beatable, but as in years past, we had beaten ourselves. We had registered on the map as a Top 25 team only to blip back off. We all just sat there stunned and tried to forget what had just happened.

▶ OFF THE RECORD

Hugs and Kisses

After a loss in high school, whether anyone will admit it, the best remedy was some affection from mom. There is something about a mom's hug that seems to make the day a little brighter. But now that I was in college my mom was 5,000 miles away. It was Senior Night, when all the seniors are honored following the final home game of the season. I didn't want to walk out; I was ashamed we had lost. I didn't deserve to be honored. Besides, Senior Night seemed to be more for the local players. I didn't have any family at the game, and my friends were all on the team. I thought I could skip out—sneak out the back without anyone noticing. I tried, but Coach George Lumpkin, in his priceless, exasperated tone of voice, said, "Come on son, put your jersey back on. Get out there." Before I knew it, I heard, "Ian Sample" over the stadium speakers.

I slowly walked down the ramp to where the tunnel opened up onto the field and was greeted with thousands of cheers. Everyone was screaming and yelling. I thought to myself, "Surely they called Leonard's name or maybe Samson's. These fans don't know who I am." I shook Coach Jones' hand as he handed me a plaque. He spoke in my ear; something about me being one of the finest players. I shrugged it off. It was something he had to say; he's probably told hundreds of seniors before me the same thing. One of the girls who worked in the athletic office gave me the obligatory, University of Hawai'i-issued lei and I posed for a quick picture.

I turned around and was going to cheer for the next player and then find my way back inside the locker room. Then a bunch of the players and their families stopped me and gave me leis. I thought it was nice of them to buy leis for all the seniors. I met some parents and was impressed with how grateful they seemed. After the pleasantries with friends, and family of friends, my attention turned back toward the locker room. There was nothing better than some heavy sulking and self-loathing right after a tough loss, and I needed a quiet place to do it. I saw a couple freshmen sneak back in, and I quickly followed. As I slyly slipped past the hordes of people I felt a light tug on my jersey. I looked down and saw a little kid who wanted me to sign his shirt. I bent over and signed my name. I thanked him, as I always did because I felt that it was more of a privilege for me to autograph something than it was for someone to receive my signature. He stared at me blankly so I gave him a slight smile. I looked up to see where those clever little freshmen went, but I still felt this little kid's eyes boring holes into my face. I looked down again and gave him another, rather sheepish smile.

Then a local couple walked up to us and said to the boy, "What do you say?" I looked down at him and, still winning the staring contest, he said, "Thaaank youuuu." I laughed—I couldn't help it. His parents took a picture of the two of us. They shook my hand and thanked me for playing a great game. I said thanks, and as they walked away I wondered if they'd been watching the same game. Quickly, my attention turned back to my getaway, but just as I was about to sneak behind the security guard and go back to the locker room, I remembered that my girlfriend's parents were at the game and I was supposed to meet them in the stands right by our sideline. Damn it, so close.

I returned to the sideline where hundreds of people stood and hung over the rail for player signatures and photo ops. I spotted her family and went over to greet them. Suddenly, I was being mobbed by autograph-hungry fans. I had signed autographs before so it wasn't a big deal but these complete strangers covered me with leis and compliments. They said things like, "Great job, Ian." "You have been so exciting to watch." I looked on in amazement, it wasn't that I never experienced fanfare before but people had never been so quick to recognize me. Mind you, I had on my No. 3 jersey with "Sample" embroidered on the back, but you could tell by the tone in their voices they were more than just run-of-the-mill fans. They were more intimate with me. I could tell these were the fans that watched *The June Jones Show* on TV and knew about my struggles in trying to play football. These were the people who read *The Honolulu Advertiser* and the *Honolulu Star-Bulletin* and knew I was an English major who aspired to get a book published. On top of all the "congratulations" and "good jobs," they told me things like, "I hope your mom is doing okay," and "Let me know when you're done with your novel."

The sincerity in their voices moved me. They looked at me as if I was a close friend. To them I was a family member who entered their homes and hearts every Saturday. I stayed in their minds until they had the chance to watch the team play again. They truly were fans of the game, UH football and me. While all along I thought I played for myself and my team, I was actually playing for these people. Coach Jones always said that we represented Hawai'i but I pegged that as just another tired way of saying, "Play hard; play respectfully." It wasn't till that day that I really understood what he meant. These fans had an investment in our team, one that wasn't financial but emotional.

One couple handed me a shirt and said, "You deserve this." I unfolded the shirt and it read, "Respect the Locals." I knew how much local people protected their culture and identity. The shirt, from complete strangers, meant I passed some kind of test. I was privileged to be considered, if only by two people, local. Kids asked for pictures and girls wanted group photos with friends. One girl even freaked out, like I was some teen idol. She shook from head to toe with excitement and her eyes started to glaze over with tears.

Here's how my teammates described our connection with Hawai'i and its fans:

"Hawai'i is a different environment and lifestyle. You can look at life in a whole other way," Davone said. "It's definitely better (than home) because it mellows you, it lets you just live life. Everybody is just so nice and it brings the good out in you."

And from Nate: "The fans have always been there for me, from when Nate was 180 pounds to when Nate was 250 pounds. I don't have a big enough thank-you for them."

That night, those fans didn't care that we lost. They didn't even care that we fell short of our own expectations. They knew better than I did that it was about more than just a game. It had little to do with wins and losses. Those loyal fans, the ones that go to games and watch religiously on TV, knew something that we as players need to be reminded of in tough times: that it's not how many times you get tackled or go home bruised and beaten. It's the understanding that we are willing to do it again, day after day, week after week, season after season because we are, in the best definition, with the utmost pride—Warriors.

▶ IN THE LOCKER ROOM

A special thanks to the "Warriors" who never suit up …

To Brian

"Rain or shine, he's out on the field. And if he's not there, he's eating with us or up in the coach's office helping with the computers. He never misses a practice—that's dedication."

"He's a man of few words but you can tell he cares about UH football. If it was just a game to him he wouldn't be there every day cheering us on."

To John "The Mailman" and Guy

"Both John and Guy are like coaches. They help us with our practices and sometimes even give us pointers. Might as well give them a whistle and an office."

"Not a lot is known about them other than the fact that they genuinely like helping us out. Guy is out there every day catching and tossing balls around. This man, who must be in his 60s or 70s, rides his bike to practice, gets there earlier than some of the players just to help out. And he stays after practice to continue to work with our guys. He sees each one of us grow as both players and people. Then we leave. It's easy to dismiss someone like this but they are there because they have a deep passion for football, and for us Warriors. I see him every morning throwing with Davone, and warming up some of the new guys. When I first walked on, he was the first person I talked to. I remember that I wasn't cleared to play yet so all I could do was watch practice. He was the first person to come up to me and offer to throw the ball around.

And don't let his age fool you because he can throw some bullets. He was honestly the first real Warrior I met. I came all the way from Jersey, and Guy was the first one to show me what aloha really means."

Uncle Cliff

"The best masseuse that money can buy. Lucky for us, he's free. If you've got a bruise, break, fracture, cramp or tear, Uncle Cliff is your guy. He will volunteer his time and effort and come in early morning after practice to help work out your injuries. Of course you will have to wait in line behind Leonard Peters, because somehow he is always first. But Uncle Cliff takes care of anyone who needs some healing. The worst part of the massage isn't when he's breaking up knots or even the feel of the IcyHot burning your skin, it's when he pats your back and says, Okay, all done."

"He comes in and helps any of us out. It doesn't matter if you're a rookie or senior. After a massage all you want is to knock out for the day. He's the reason I missed so many classes."

Other fans

"We just got done running gassers at the end of practice, and I was sitting beside the fence catching my breath when this man came up to me. I figured he wanted me to sign something so I put down my helmet and stood up. As he came over I noticed he had some kind of figurine in his hand. He handed me a model football player and said, "Thank you so much for such a great season." I asked him if he wanted me to sign it, but he said it was for me. I told him thanks and he walked away. I looked down at what I had in my hand and it was a football player version of me! It had my skin color down, and our away uniform completely perfect. It even had the triangle patterns of our sleeves and pants. I found out that this man made models for a lot of the starters. Playing this game in Hawai'i, you don't realize how many people you affect and touch. I was blown away. I called my mom up and told her I finally had an action figure!"

"I remember it was the day after the Purdue game. I went into a place down in Waikiki just for a bite to eat by myself. I ordered Chicken Tenders and a burger, I think. Halfway through the meal the waiter told me, "Good game." I just said "thank you," but I was surprised he even knew who I was because we're always wearing helmets. There are great people out there, not just groupies and people who jump on the bandwagon. There are true fans of football and, more so, Hawaiʻi football. It makes playing so much more meaningful when something like that happens. That day I was prouder than ever to represent something so worthwhile."

CHAPTER 15

ARIZONA STATE SUN DEVILS

▶ OFF THE FIELD

Bowl Week—Let the Festivities Begin!

The start of Bowl Week meant several things—money, games and free time. We were up in the Sheraton Moana Surfrider hotel for a week before the Sheraton Hawai'i Bowl. The seniors had the best rooms with a view to die for—beach, sunsets and babes. To add excitement to the week we were in the heart of Waikiki, with no curfews until game night. Each night there was something mandatory. Certain nights we had to attend luaus and other special events. During the day there might be a trip to Hilo Hattie for discounted shopping, or a visit to Hawaiian Waters Adventures Park to play around in the water.

But what we really looked forward to was spending our bowl money, which was about $200. We also looked forward to getting the bowl gifts. We got Oakley backpacks and trinkets like mini-helmets. We got towels, collared shirts and T-shirts. They gave us specially-made watches and sunglasses with a built-in MP3 player worth about $300. But our biggest gift, the one we got on the last day of the week, is what we called the "senior gift." The seniors have the luxury of picking out one item to get for the entire team. Usually we had between $200–$300 to spend on each player.

The seniors wanted to give everyone the latest video game console, XBOX 360, but it wasn't within our budget. We got together and juggled a few ideas. Digital cameras were the best buy. Most of us didn't own one, and if we did, we could either trade or sell it, plus it would make for a great Christmas present for the family. That was what Bowl Week was about—prizes, money and fun. Oh, we practiced, too, in the mornings with the same old routine. School was between semesters, and some of us had already graduated, so we had a lot of down time.

Bowl Week also meant it was time to grind! We went to Outback Steakhouse, attended luaus, buffets—all-around great eating. The only drawback was that most of our dinners were spent with the Arizona State team. It was somewhat awkward seeing them around all the time. I wasn't sure if that was an ideal situation. We saw the faces behind the team that we wanted to kill. In fact, tensions built so fast between our two teams that the "friendly" kick-off dinner almost became the biggest Sun Devil beating in the history of their program. What got our blood boiling and fists clenched? In order to explain that I'm going to take you back, way back, to the night I was lying on my undersized cot during summer camp ...

The Haka

All the football players were bunked in two dance studios for August's summer camp with nothing more than one small cot, two pillows, one sheet and one bedspread per player. I was in Studio 2 with the rest of the seniors and the entire football freshman class. The rest of the team was in Studio 1. Hardly anyone was in my studio that night; everyone seemed to be swarming to what was going on in Studio 1. I figured someone got into a fight or maybe there was some big Madden game going on. I lay back down and dove right back into *The Giver,* one of the many books on my fall reading list. I wasn't but two sentences into it when I heard loud stomping coming from the other room, I put down my book and jogged over to see what the commotion was. Lo and behold, I saw 30 to 40 guys with their shirts off, sweating, doing some sort of strange dance. Actually, I wouldn't have called it a dance. It was more like a fraternity step, but it was something I've never seen before. I laughed at first—the guys were sticking out their tongues and making their eyes big. It was a sight to see. I sat down and asked Ross Dickerson what was going on. "Tala and Leonard are teaching us the haka," he told me.

"What's a haka?" I asked. Before he could respond his shirt was off and he joined the rest of the team. I figured it was some local thing. Most of us Mainlanders were merely watching.

"Come on, Ian, get in," Chad Mock said. I just laughed and said, "No, thank you." To be quite honest, I felt like it was something only the local guys should be doing. And frankly, I didn't get the point of it.

That night I remained a spectator. I watched Tala and Leonard teach the players the movements of this Maori dance from New Zealand. It only took one or two tries before the guys caught on to a segment of the dance, then Leonard would add more steps to the routine. As they learned the body movements, they were also taught the words, "Ki runga ki te rangi ..."

Bed check was at 11 p.m. and most of the dance was put into place. The guys, sweating and out of breath, went back to their cots. I lay back down and told myself that next time they practiced, I was going to be front and center. I knew nothing of the haka's history or its meaning. All I knew was that my teammates were doing it and I wanted to be a part of it. The next day after morning practice the words to the haka chant were posted in our locker room. I asked Leonard, plain and simple, what is the haka? What is it for? He told me it was a war chant performed by Maori warriors to intimidate their enemies before going into battle. But, he explained further, "The haka isn't really I'm going to come over and bash your head in. It's basically saying, This is my land and I'm going to protect it, so if you want to come over here and do something, you're going to get it."

Later that day I saw Samson Satele and a bunch of the O-line huddled around a monitor in the computer lab. They were watching video clips of New Zealand's rugby team, the All-Blacks, performing the haka. Holy shit! I wouldn't want to play them. Sharing my sentiment was the opposing team. Fear and awe highlighted their shocked faces as the All-Blacks stomped and shouted in their native tongue. Talk about intimidation!

That night most of the team, including myself, learned the haka movements and words. The next day we performed it for the coaches and other spectators. It was something else. When we all did it together, we were like one giant body. The energy that flowed through us was like none other. Even just practicing it pumped adrenaline through our veins. I swear it was like no other feeling I've experienced. The haka made each person part of something greater.

I asked Leonard whose idea it was to do the haka. He said that Coach Jones came to him and Tala and asked them to do something to unite the team, and he suggested the haka.

To me, the haka wasn't special because of its history or tradition; rather it was the fact that it was ours. The only way I can describe it is that if we were truly at war, fighting against perilous odds, then I would stand on the front line with a smile, knowing that I have 100 of my Warriors with me. It didn't matter if my teammate standing beside me was from California or Hawai'i, Seattle or Houston. The Warriors were ready to go to war with anyone who dared to step in our way. The haka wasn't about fear or intimidation. To me, it was about trust and brotherhood. It wasn't about frightening the other team; it was about knowing that we weren't going to be scared—not here, not now, not ever!

For something like this to really work, it has to come from the heart and soul of the program—the guys who put their bodies on the line for their sport. For us, it was a war chant to be performed before games or after great victories, whenever *we* all felt the need and desire for it.

But as the haka gained attention in the media, many of us felt that something we took so much pride in was slipping from our grasps and into the hands of the sports marketers, who sell everything from videos to logo wear. Now it was becoming a show. Coach Jones announced that they planned to film it and put music behind it and make a DVD. Our proud haka was becoming a 100-man traveling act. We could have opened for Celine Dion in Vegas! Once we even had to perform it after a loss. It was sickening to see something so great take such a turn.

Before the Sheraton Hawai'i Bowl, we did the haka just for *us* one last time. The team was at the kickoff dinner held two nights before the game. The Warriors and the ASU Sun Devils were eating in the same banquet hall. The dinner opened up with Arizona State's cheerleaders dancing and cheering, performing their fight song. Then our cheerleaders and a couple band members came into the room and did Hawai'i's cheer. They started playing the theme from *Hawai'i Five-0,* so some of the guys got up on their chairs, including Coach Jeff Reinebold, and started the patented rowing motion. (This motion is done by many fans simultaneously with this tune. It's also done at UH volleyball and basketball games.)

We waved our green napkins in the air as school spirit swept through us. Looking through the waving hands and green napkins twirling, I spotted yellow twirling napkins at the far end of the room. Apparently, ASU didn't want to be upstaged by our fanatic display of school pride so they started to wave their colors, too. When the band stopped, one of the Sun Devils led his team into a chant of their own. They turned toward us and began clapping and yelling out some unified clap routine. It wasn't too impressive, but the mere fact that they taunted us from only a couple feet away got us going. We were riled up. Those of us who were seated suddenly stood up, and the teams stared each other down. It broke out into a yelling and name-calling match. Then Tala stood up on a chair and yelled with all his might, "Taringa whakarongo! Kia rite! Kia rite! Kia mau!" The team yelled back to him, "Hiiiiiiii," with a powerful, collective stomp. We shouted and danced the haka that night like we were the greatest warriors who ever set foot in Hawai'i. By the time it was over most of the ASU players were too scared to look our way. The host of the evening quickly ran to the mic and tried to reduce the tension. I looked over at Coach Jones who was wearing a smile on his face. I knew he was proud to see what our team had become. It didn't matter if we were on or off the field; we were Warriors all the same. We forced ourselves to take our seats. I sat down and looked at my fellow receivers, all of us were shaking, hands trembling. Adrenaline had taken complete control and we did our best to calm our nerves. That night was the last time I did the haka. And I pray that future warriors will know the value and the meaning behind this Polynesian dance that so affected a mulatto kid from Jersey.

Following the Yellow Brick Road

So now we're back to where I began this narrative: the Sheraton Hawai'i Bowl on Dec. 24, 2006. Halftime had passed. Coach Jones had already ended my college football career and my Warrior team was on its way to winning our final game of the season. I sat feeling abandoned and desolate on the bench. Like Dorothy in *The Wizard of Oz*, I felt like the entire season, with all of its struggles and successes with my friends, was just a dream.

My friends and I were all swept up away from our homes in California, Seattle and New Jersey and plopped down in a far-off place that I sometimes think of as the Emerald City—the University of Hawai'i. There we were told by little menehune and a big coach to follow the yellow brick road. We spent years following that road, the only road there is and the only road we know. Along the way we overcame obstacles and trials. We faced our fears and horrors. We made friends—some courageous, some wise, others foolish, but all ambitious. Not one of us was strong enough to walk alone, but together we made our way down that yellow brick road. Occasionally we'd reach out to each other to reassure ourselves that we were still there.

At last we reach the gates of the Emerald City and come face to face with the great Wizard of Oz. You want him to give you all the answers. But the more you learn, the more you realize that the Wizard is no magician after all, but just a man like any other—although one who controls your life from school to football (which leaves little room for anything else). And for the four or five years you may be on the team, he is still the one person you always look to for approval.

It's extremely hard to step outside the box and look in. To try and analyze the player-coach relationship is impossible, especially when our livelihoods are so entwined within it. But if a player does have the clarity of vision (or later on, 20/20 hindsight) it's far easier to see. The head coach—Coach Jones—is in to do one thing—win. The same goal we as players have. Questions of fairness and politics aren't asked after a win because they don't matter. For Coach Jones it would be impossible to please a hundred players, all his coaches and the thousands of fans. Impossible. He wins the best way he knows how. He makes decisions based on what he thinks the team needs. And although the players, the University or the press might strongly disagree with his stance or means of going about a certain something, the fact of the matter is when all's said and done, when the dust settles and the day is over, he is the sole person responsible for everything that goes on. Blame will fall squarely on his shoulders and his shoulders alone.

Coach Jones ended my collegiate career, but we went on to win our final game 41-24. It took me months to understand or even admit it, but in the end the team won—my team won—the only thing that will ever matter.

CHAPTER 16

WHEN ALL IS NOT SAID AND DONE

Should I Stay or Should I Go?

I woke up the other day, brushed my teeth and walked into the kitchen. I opened the freezer and found myself faced with a difficult decision—frozen pizza or waffles? I went with the waffles. They were the blueberry kind; who could resist? That was the toughest decision I made all day.

My choices were easy ones. My decision didn't make a difference of millions of dollars. I could only imagine being a 23-year-old kid, playing two seasons of college football and then having to make a decision whether to leave school early or throw my helmet into the ring for the NFL draft. The high stakes included a possible first-round pick and a signing bonus of at least a couple million.

Colt Brennan had to make that kind of decision. Some analysts said, "Go to the NFL. School will always be there. Take the money." Others disagreed: "Stay in college football one more year. Get stronger, faster, better. It will mean more money later." Personally, I was happy when Colt announced in the spring of 2007 that he was going to stay. Even though I had graduated and was no longer a Warrior, I knew how much the team needed him. He was our general, our commander, our leader. With Colt on the team I knew my friends had another shot at the WAC title and a Bowl Championship Series game. It meant that Davone, Ryan and Jason would have another all-star, record-breaking year. But most important, it meant Hawai'i had another chance to watch the finest quarterback I've ever played with, in action for one more year.

I sat down with Colt one day in the spring and asked him, "Why did you turn down the NFL? I mean, the money would have been in the millions. Why did you stay in the Islands?" He explained, "In Hawai'i you get to experience an unique atmosphere. Hawai'i is its own thing and if you can respect it, it can be something really fun. I stayed because I felt

I'd be comfortable here for another year. Considering how we ended last season, with all the momentum and enthusiasm out there, my decision was much easier."

I reminded him that the NFL meant millions; it was a chance very few people got. How did he turn that down? Once again, he made it seem far simpler than I had imagined: "Down deep inside I wanted to play in the NFL. I worked for it since I was a kid. I never would have imagined it would go this way. But what I have out here is a chance to live life differently, a more enjoyable life. Hopefully in a year I'll still have a chance to go the NFL. It's a win-win."

I thought about what Colt said it being a "win-win." How couldn't it be? Stay in paradise for another year, then continue on and play big-league football. It's crazy to think about it, but in a couple of years I will know more than a dozen people in the NFL. Colt, Davone, Jason, Samson, Nate, Tala—the list goes on. But I won't just know them, I mean I will really know them. They will be the guys I could call up and invite over for a family barbecue. The ones I'd invite to my wedding, and the ones I'd expect to throw me a bachelor party!

After talking with Colt, I realized that we all have choices to make. Granted some are riskier than others. Mine was to write this book. I chose to put football aside for a while and become what I hoped would be the one voice of hundreds of players. The same voice that failed to fulfill my promise to tell my Warriors what they all really mean to me.

My Farewell Speech to my Teammates

Football, shit, it's a hell of a game. Truly a game like no other. No one person can win it. It takes a team. Vince Lombardi, one of the most successful coaches in football, once said:

"Every time a football player goes to play his trade he's got to play from the ground up—from the soles of his feet right up to his head. Every inch of him has to play. Some guys play with their heads. That's OK. You've got to be smart to be No. 1 in any business. But more importantly, you've got to play with your heart, with every fiber of your body. If you're lucky enough to find a guy with a lot of head and a lot of heart, he's never going to come off the field second."

Yeah we lost some games, we weren't perfect. But no one ever asked us to be. Vince had it right: "you've got to play with your heart." Football—I don't love it. There were times in my college-playing career when I didn't want anything to do with it. But that never stopped me from stepping onto that field every day with you and playing with everything I owned.

And I know that winning is the ultimate goal. Without wins we'd have nothing to show for our blood, sweat and tears. But wins don't come easy without trust. That's what playing great is about—trust. When I ran down that field I knew, I trusted that Colt would put that ball right where I needed it. I trusted the O-line to block and give Colt the time, and when I ran after the catch I knew my receivers would do everything in their power to block for me. That is what winning is. When I walked off to the sideline, I knew that our defense would hit with every ounce of heart they had. I trusted them to be relentless. I trusted them to endure. I trusted them because I knew that was what it took to win. And if one of us made a mistake, it didn't matter because I had faith that they would do everything they could to be better on the next down. Winning isn't about one player getting the post-game interview or game ball. It's about every single one of us being Warriors.

And what is a warrior? Someone who shows courage, who shows bravery? That's a pretty good definition, but it leaves becoming a warrior open to almost anybody. What that definition lacks is where and how warriors are made. They are made right here on this island. They are made on this soil beneath our feet. In no other place do more warriors assemble than here. Descendants of the great kingdoms of Tonga, Samoa, Hawai'i. The descendants of great African kings. The legendary tribes of Saxons, Native Americans and Far East dynasties all gather here. We convene in the most remote place on earth and forge wars against whoever dares to challenge who we are and what we stand for! We strip away differences and fight side by side because we know that immortality resides in the record books. This is not a game; this is our lives!

Football is played on a hostile battlefield. The opponent tries to steal my will to win, to cut my legs out from under me. And there will be days when he will win and I'll fall bullied and broken. But even when the opponent claims the victory, he will never take away my will to fight! I have learned to battle till my legs can no longer hold me, till my knuckles are bare to the bone, till my lungs have given up their fight to inhale. And I know that with my very last breath I will leave this world tall and proud because once I was a Warrior!

Aloha

A special word to my receivers: I have to watch the games over again to really remember what it was like—the cheers, the screams, the fanfare. Those parts were good, but they were only the milieu. What I look for when I watch the games are the slaps on the helmet after a good catch. What I've noticed is that every one of us searched for the player who scored, so we could jump high and celebrate with him. Ryan, I remember waiting with Chad Mock in the end zone after your first touchdown since you were off injured reserve. Waiting for you to finish praying just so we could say, "Welcome back, great job, let's keep it going," even if all it really was was a high five or a slap on the shoulder. Chad, I remember jumping higher than you after you scored that touchdown against Louisiana Tech, just because I loved seeing you get the opportunity to make something happen. I remember the bets we made in the locker room—whoever had the biggest block in the game got $5 dollars from everyone. We didn't care who scored touchdowns or who had the most yards in a game; we wanted to see who had the best block for another receiver. It was a privilege to play with you, Davone and Ryan, the way you juke out defenders always struck me with awe. I remember thinking, "Next play, if I get the ball I'm going to run through a defender like Ross and Jason do."

Every one of us will move on to bigger and better things, but before we do, I need to say thank you. I was always the quiet one, laughing and smiling nearly every day when I was around you guys. Jason, you'd call me Gums, because they always showed when I laughed. And I don't know how many times Davone got on me for always smiling or chuckling about something. And because I was never a huge talker, I was never quite sure if you knew what you all meant to me. At clubs I'd wait for a fight to break out so I'd have a chance to show my dedication, my loyalty to you guys. In the game I'd pray that I'd have the opportunity to throw a big block, especially against a lineman or linebacker so you'd see what I'd put on the line for one of you. But that chance never came and already a new season has begun.

In the years to come, some of us will grow apart and fade away. I guess that's only natural. But whatever you're doing come five, 10 years or more, know that you had a teammate and a friend, whose loyalty will remain as timeless as these words. Thank you.

EPILOGUE

In the months following the incredible 2006 season, we seniors began to go our separate ways. An unprecedented five UH Warriors were selected in the 2007 National Football League draft. Ikaika Alama-Francis and Samson Satele were drafted in the second round. Ikaika went to the Detroit Lions and Samson to the Miami Dolphins. In the sixth round Regan Mauia was also picked up by the Dolphins and Mel Purcell was drafted by the Cleveland Browns. And Nate Ilaoa was drafted in the seventh round by the Philadelphia Eagles. Other seniors signed as free agents: Tala Esera joined Samson and Regan in Miami, Kenny Patton went to the Oakland Raiders, Leonard Peters to the New York Jets, Dane Uperesa to the Cincinnati Bengals and Lawrence Wilson to the Baltimore Ravens. It was the best year ever for UH seniors in the NFL.

Of course, there's more to getting drafted than just having a good season and then waiting around for a pro team to call. After the season is over, draft prospects must train hard and perform to the best of their ability at a "combine" of NFL scout and coaches. At a combine you run the 40-yard dash, bench press, scamper through cones, jump high, jump far and execute countless drills. The scouts critique your every move and jot down notes on everything from the length of your hands to the shape of your butt.

Some of the seniors went to Texas or Arizona to receive combine training. But thanks to the efforts of Jon Neilsen, a former pro football player and a good friend of the Warrior program, a handful of us were able to train with the Speedburners program run by coach Rick Hagedorn in Orange County, California. In a matter of weeks Rick's coaching had me running a 4.32 40-yard dash, Ross flying through shuttle drills and Leonard exploding out of a standing start. We were all grateful for the professional training and eager to show off the results at the NFL combine.

Of course, preparation alone can't determine how you perform on a single day. While one guy shines at the combine, the next guy can have an off day. So when the draft finally rolled around on the last weekend in April, many of us were picked up and given a shot to play in the NFL. But those of us who weren't immediately chosen had some thinking to do: How important was it to chase the dream, and how long would we chase it?

Athletes who play college sports with no real professional potential are lucky; after their final season there are no expectations about playing at a higher level. But football players are different. We're often expected to at least try to play professionally, although most of us lack either the motivation or the skills—or both. Many of us enjoy college football for all that it's worth but don't love it enough to make it a full-time job. We have lived and breathed football for years and have hardly had a chance to think about the alternatives.

So what does life hold for those of us who have happily given up the pro football dream—either temporarily or for good? Well Marques Kaonohi spent lots more time surfing the beaches around Oʻahu. Ross Dickerson started looking into culinary school and the police academy. Chad Mock was enjoying the laid-back Hawaiʻi lifestyle, mostly at the beach, until football jumped right back into his life and he signed with the British Columbia Lions of the Canadian Football League.

As for me, I made the decision to put football aside for a while. For months I was able to switch football mode off and just relax for the first time in a long time—no pressure, no stress. The world—and especially Hawaiʻi—was now my oyster. I spent my days going to beaches I had only heard my classmates talk about. I went diving and snorkeling and learned how to surf. And I spent my nights at the computer, furiously typing to finish this book.

And then, with the sand still between my toes and the manuscript barely off to the publisher, football came calling again. I was offered a chance to play for Big Blue, a professional team run by IBM Japan in that country's X League. And before I knew it, I was on my way to Tokyo.

Just like that, the game had reminded me that it still had a firm hold on my life—at least for the time being.

I am, after all, a football player.

Sayonara!

ABOUT THE AUTHOR

New Jersey native J. Ian Sample epitomizes the man who follows the road less traveled. After dropping out of his first college, the University of Delaware, in 2001 he made his way across the country to Honolulu, where he joined the University of Hawaiʻi football team as a walk-on. As a senior he was one of the Hawaiʻi Warriors' star wide receivers, catching 10 of the 58 touchdown catches that broke the NCAA single-season record. In December 2006 he graduated with a B.A. in English and is currently living and playing professional football in Japan. *Once a Warrior* is his first book, which he plans to follow with a screenplay. He can be reached at once_warrior@yahoo.com.